LEOTHWORC

A collection of eighty poems

Lëaf Ednïwinga Eardmor

PublishAmerica
Baltimore

First printing

PublishAmerica has allowed this work to remain exactly as the author intended, verbatim, without editorial input.

Hardcover 978-1-4560-2008-8
Softcover 978-1-4560-2007-1
PUBLISHED BY PUBLISHAMERICA, LLLP
www.publishamerica.com
Baltimore

Printed in the United States of America

Lëaf I am
upon leaves I pen
my fame to win

Lëaf Ic eom
Uppan Leafum ic feþer
Mín mærnes to earne

This book is dedicated with love to my sweetheart Jonathan
--Lëaf

Note to the fair reader:

My dear reader, this is a collection of my work, save for small bits which I have gathered from elsewhere, such as the costermonger's calls in the children's section, which are real old street calls from London. The dusty Miller poem, Lady Wind, and Fraiser's Elegy of the Quack doctor are all my own adaptations of old rhymes.

All else is wholly my own original work.

There are also some instances where the Anglo-Saxon language appears, largely in translation.

I enjoy coining and inventing words, so beware. No worries, however, for I provide explanatory footnotes.

Contents

HIGH POETRY

Living—a reflection on mortality

These solitary verses I pen,
So that you will know that once, I lived and breathed—
As sure as you are breathing now.

Though still my breast lies now,
Stilled the heart that used to beat,
And long since ceased
The hand that held this pen.
Cheeks on which roses used to bloom
Eyes in which stars used to shine.
Once, my laugh was heard.
Though they forget my name,
I thought and lived, all the same.
And I felt the bitter-sweetness—
Pangs of love, hate, despair and sorrow
But followed for me a brighter tomorrow.

Mortal are we, dust granted
But a breath of life;
A short waking hour,
Like a rain-beaten flower,
To make itself known
And then be swallowed
Back up into the abyss.
Though our souls live eternal
For good or ill –the mighty hand
Of Death our hearts doth still.
Only if we hold the key—
Behind held out for all who will see
Now I quietly lie beneath some aged green tree
But you can be assured that once I lived—as sure as you live now
As did all who beneath the green earth now lie—
We live, we breathe, we love, and then we die.

Hail to the peace-weaver!

She driveth away wrath
And bringeth forth peace to her house and all within.
Hail to the Peace-weaver!
She is the loaf-maker! She is the key-keeper!
She is the fair queen of the golden mead-hall!
She gives out her lord's rings, gold and silver in the mead-hall
and goes forth bearing sweet ale to the guests. They delight in
her presence, and adore her beauty.
She is strong and noble, being fair and beautiful,
And worthy of her kin's loyalty.
She sends off her brave men to battle, singing the war song,
handing them their silver spears.
A shield-maiden, a noble peace-weaver of her house!
Hail to the shield-maiden,
Her children will honor her when she is grey.
Her husband and her house
Shall be blessed forever because of her.
Hail to the peace-weaver!
Hail to the glorious woman!
She supports her husband, her king!
She listens when he plans.
She laughs when he laughs.
She weeps when he weeps.
She labors to grind his bread,
Working her fair hands to the bone
For her Lord and her children.
Will they be grateful?
She is clothed all in brown garments,
But when she is old they will wash her
And dress her in gold and fine raiment,
And put in her hair a crown of flowers,
For she is their queen.
Hail to the peace-weaver,
For she is great among her folk,
And high in the eyes of heaven!

The Seed Song

I

Hark! Small seed, lift up thy head,
Stir with life; feel the warmth
Sift down to thy darkling bed.
Fashioned from the first
To fall in love with light
Yet thou wilt need new eyes
Before thou canst have true sight.
A beautiful and gentle heart have thee, a gift so very rare.
A plan of purest grace for thy fortune is conceived
By the gracious one who sowed thee there.
The perfect reward waits for those who have believed.

II

Soft and secret, in the dark of night,
Making not the silkiest sound,
The wisest of the wise
One day thou shalt confound.
There is great promise in thy tiny self
Humble though thou be
Who knows that in thy secret heart
Thou longs to be a tree?
Deep in thy soul pure and bright
Thou remembers the flickering light
From endless suns long ago.
Liberated from the bonds of earth,
Pushing on to the day; bending to and fro.

III

Thy hope is the only thing that sustains,
A hope that one day thou will see the light
And leave dark earth and fell shade behind.
But breaking free seems a vain dream;
Of days dim and far away it's but a gleam.
Yet take heart, and courage!
They will aid thee on thy way;
Thy simple faith will bear thee
When thy reasoning will sway.
For the small and weak things of the world
Have been chosen to confound the wise all along,
And the humble and foolish things
Have been chosen to bewilder the strong.
Thou was not called to remain in the earth
But to rise above it and do great things
One day all will see the truth;
From the lowliest beggars to mighty kings.

IV

Many are called, but few are chosen.
Though thou resideth in it,
Thou art not of this place:
Thou art not part of the darkness,
But a piece of purest grace.
Thou wast called by that great light
And forth thou shalt hasten,
To depart from the night!
Arise! Lift up thy head
Reach up, press on towards the sky.
Thou wast not called to stay in bed!
How can thou grow if thou will not try?

V

Felt at last; like relief of rain; the joy of breaking free.
Peace floods through thy leaves, made known are secrets
That before thou couldst not see
Truth now clear that once was dim
Joy and life flow through every limb
Of thou, the finished tree.
Pain and tears have passed away,
Only love and joy remain.
Hope is gone, and so is faith
Faded like the sun on the last day
They are not needed more,
As at the ending of all things
Gone are all the earthly kings
So runs the ancient lore.
Sorrow is a stranger here,
A half-echo of long ago
So hasten to come a-planting with me
And seeds of joy we'll sow.

A-roving

A-roving I go
Past stone and river's flow
And long has it been since
We have seen our dear hearth and home
Since we passed by stock or stone
Ever on and on, alone.
Over hill and under dale
Oh hear the mountains song so hale
See the rocks all pale
Long has it been since my home I saw
Or heard the laugh of the jackdaw
May I wander a little further, and then,
Go back over the old road to find my home again.
And ever may I
Look out upon the hills
And hear the brook that
From the mountains spills.
And when I am old
And have seen many a Midsummer year
May my old heart never fear
To set my feet to the road once more
To see what it holds in store
For there may be yet a hidden road
Or gold in a bold mountain stowed
By forgotten folk for me to find
So let the road onward wind
And round the green hedge there may be still
A new path or a secret rill.

Elegy for Eadgyth

Notes: This work was composed to be read aloud in Old English at the reburial of Anglo-Saxon Princess Eadgyth, in Germany, October 22, 2010. There are several kennings present in this work. Kennings are miniature word-riddles; for example, the compound word *'whale-road'* is a kenning for 'the sea'. The verse heading numbers include the Anglo-Saxon name for the number, then the Modern English number in roman numerals. The complete Anglo-Saxon translation appears at the conclusion of the Modern English poem.

An: I

Eadgyth, Ah, Eadgyth
Loveliest princess of the south
Mistress of the hearth and heath
Hail to the Peace-weaver!
She was the loaf-maker!
She was the key-keeper!
Hail, fair Eadgyth!
Giver of gifts,
A gracious lady in the hall,
Bestowing prudent words and bringing valor and joy
Wisdom and a sturdy hand employ.
A Peace-weaver strong, a boon to all who knew her
Great was thy father, elder and wise was he
Thy mother Ælfflæd; a noble woman was she
Accustomed to graceful actions in field and hall.
Thou sprung from the greatest kings the land ever knew
They did noble and famous deeds in that country
Endeavors soon fated to be forgotten by latter men.
The blood of great kings flowed once in thy veins
Alfred the great was thy grandsire.
Now thy blood, like royal wine runneth
In the veins of every noble house
Upon this great continent.
Old stories still sing of thy bravery,
Thy skill, Thy doughtiness,
womanly strength incarnate
Highly esteemed,
Like a gem among the people
Calm were thy ways,
Thou glowed with charm
Yet banished with thy mother,
When but a maid

In Salisbury thou stay'd.
In chalky Wessex reared.
Thy queenly fate brought thee to Germany at tender age
As oft are the duties of great queens; they must be valiant.

Twegen: II

Words of love once whispered into an ivory ear
Bonds of wedlock promised; flowers on the marriage bed
Held thou sway over distant lands, thy faith unmarred by fear;
A noble queen to rule with queenly stead.
Two children thou bore thy king
To be the heir-treasures of two noble lands.
A famous man-warrior, a duke,
A fair maiden too, thou bore
Strove to keep them safe from pain and war.
Thou sent fierce fighters off to battle
Offering them their silver spears
To chant with iron-hard voices in the spear-din.
Singing the war-song loud and clear
And days passed away when skillful scops
Would tell tales of old, echoing
As river-music in the joyful hall;
At the dawning of the famous English realm
Of gleaming elder days, gold and fair trees tall
And the crowning of the aged kings
Who saw the crafting of bright corselets and mighty helm
Where the great horses leapt and lords dealt rings.
For ten winters thee and thy king
Reigned well and mightily,
Braving battles and trouble;
Yet of your deeds now few stories sing.

Þrie: III

Eadgyth, Eadgyth, has it been so very long
Since men have mourned for thee?
And when did they cease lamenting
The untimely loss of thy courageous heart?
Buried was thy flowery bed
And lost to all the eyes was the key.
In white silk wrap't
While shadows through
The great forests slowly crept
And the lives of men
Slowly playing out
Like pieces upon a board.
Whilst great battles raged and
Fiery dragons fortified their hoard.
A royal sleeping lady great
Fate sealed thy resting tomb
Frost thy earthly fetters ate.
Silk, like purest snow has been thy shroud,
Ever-veiling thee like a darkling cloud
Horns thou must have heard, as in a dream
Sounding in the deep
Lowing of bitter battles long
Disturbing not thy poisonous sleep
Angels now about thee throng.
The glorious spear-dins have long since stil'd
Loyal hearts of lords and kings are gone
Middle-earth with wicked men is fil'd
Thy cheerless passage over the whale's-way
Beyond the darkness of this mortal world
Where the greatest king of all holds sway
Has protected thee from
The mounting sorrow of this present age.

22

In time thou was lost, now we greet thee
And our homage pay thee one last time,
Ah! Our fair queen, Eadgyth!
We offer thee love as in ages past.

Feower: IV

Fair Eadgyth, Hear us now!
May thou find unending rest
At last, in the arms of
Thy good and holy eternal king
Through the darkness
Hear our last song for thee;
Our queen-gem, fair Eadgyth!
O, Eadgyth, our Peace-weaver!
Shadows, grown cold about thee fled
From thy long-quiet leaden bed
The radiance, like sunshine has found thee once again
Dispelled like mist; banished from the moors
Whither the light has flown, flood-grey;
Yet turning to gold when the sun rises.
Thy people welcome thee once more.
Thy precious bones that never saw great age
Thy silken locks that ne'er yet grew hoar.
Once again thou, our illustrious queen-lady
Reignest in our hearts, our minds adore thee
We, thy people still,
find joy in knowledge of thy happy home.
Thou departed over-soon,
Gone out the flaming light that lit
The lap of the world for so few days.
Thou kept the king's rings in plenteous quantity;
Bestowed with grace.
When first thou perished,

A flower too soon faded,
A light too soon quenched,
Thy foreign nation wept for thee
With intense sorrow,
Because thou had com'st to cherish them
With kindness and the highest love.
A bitter mourning arose in the morning.
The earth was then charged
With thy keeping, to hold thee
Until thou couldst rise again upon the last day.
Hear thee no longer
The wind in chink and stone
Nor trickle of water in pool and rill
Cold be thy hand and bone
Thy gracious heart lies still!
Brow-stars that no longer shine
A voice that no longer sings
No bright hands pouring carven cups
Full of flowing wine
Nor dealing out golden rings
Ah, Eadgyth! Fortune and Strife meet
And are hence made one.
And the potency of the latter evil
Is diminished
As if it were compared to the light of sun.
Only thou upon thy lonely bed
With no gentle king to caress thy head
Nor to crown it with flowers, white
Once gathered in the field.
A bleak honor, a joyless tribute
To wrap thy body in purest silk
And lay thee down to rest at last,
Upon thy eternal earthly couch.
Ah, Eadgyth, how long hast thou slept in the earth

Thy resting place forgotten by the eyes of men?
Alas that we should have lost thee!
Harps once struck in thy honor
Now lie in dust, unstrung.
Voices of the scops once rose in the hall
Alas that thy songs are now unsung.
Telling of great deeds of loyalty and valor
How we rejoice now at finding thee!
Be thou ever at rest again.
Now thou canst in peace forever sleep;
No warriors of old thy vigil to keep.
Eadgyth shall remain a lament
Ever-sung in the hearts of goodly men.

Anglo-Saxon Translation:

Sorglēoþ æt Eadgyth
Mearcere: Lëaf Ednïwinga Eardmor, Lȳþamonath 2010

Eadgyth, wā, Eadgyth
Cwën cȳmlicost, be sūþan
Agendfrēa heorþes ond hæþes.
Eala hæþ seo friþowebba!
Seo beon se hlǽf-dige!
Seo beon se cǽg-weard !
Eala, Eadgyth fæger!
Forgifestre giefu, se ēaþmōd forþwíf innan se meduseld,
Agifaþ Behogod wordum ond andweardaþ hildecyst ond wynn
Wīsdōm Ond ānrǽdlic hande ātēon!
Seo friþowebba stearc, se tīþ æt ǽghwæþer hwa cneów hire.
Woruldfruma sy þín fæder ealdor ond frōd beon he,
Þín módor Ælfflǽd; efenæþele wíf beon se
Willan æt gifnesfull dǽdum innan feld ond seld.

25

Eow āspringan of se besta cyningas se land ǣfre cneów.
Hit didon æþel ond brēme dǣdum innan se mearc
Hogunga tō ǣr fægera æt beon forgiten be æfterra mancynn.
Se blot fram ungeendod cyningas ærningum
Ǣne innan Þín ǣdrena
Ælfred se micel beon Þína ealdefæder.
Nú Þína blot, lice medu Cwënlic rynum
Innan se ǣdrena of ǣlc æþel hus onufan þes micel cynneard.
Eald ealdspella giet cwelÞ of Þín ellen, Þín cræft
Þína dyhtiglice, cwenlice, strengu flǣsclicnes.
Héalic blǣdāgende, cwën se gimm āmang se folc.
Hnesce beon Þína farum, eow gleowon in swētnes.
Giet āflīemed mid Þína módor Þonne ac se wynmǣg.
Innan Searoburh þé bidon.
Innan cilce Westseaxe árærde.
Eower cwenlice wyrd æt Germania ætbǣron þé on mearu
Swa oft beon se byrðenna of micel cwéne; híe sceal ácostnaþ
dǣdrōf.
Lufu-cyneworda ǣne hwisprede innan se ylpenbán-hwīt ēare.
Cospas æwnung áþweddes; blǣdnes on Þa ǣwnung-bedd
Anhealdan crýt ǣhtgeweald ofer feorland,
Eower ǣw ne-ámierede be ege.
Se æþel cwën tó rǣd in cwënlice stede.
Twēgen bearna þé begéton Þina cyning
Ǣt beon Ierfa-māþþum for twēgen æþel eardum.
Se weorþ mann-cempa, se ealdorman
Se fæger mægden éac, ácenninga þé
Efestede bewaoian híe geheald fram sār ond hild.
þé ágénsendedon gram feohtereum opfleogan tó beadu
Bringas híe hira seolfor-gúðwuda
Agalan samod īrenheard efenhléoðrung innan se gār-dyne.
Drēamnes se æscplega-swēg hlūd ond beorhtword
Ond dagas āgān hwonne scopas orþanc
Willan āreccan spella fram eald, windumæra

26

Swa ēa-glīw innan se wynnlice seld;
On se dægrēd æt se dōmlic Englisc rīce.
Æt glæmlice ealdor dagas, gold ond fæger trēowas, hēah.
Ond se gecorōnian æt se cyningas infrōd
Hwa beheóld se cræft fram byrnum beorht, ond swa helma
mihtlice
Þonne se micel horsa hléopon ond hlafords dǣl hringan.
For tīen wintreum þé ond þina cyning rícium fǣle ond mihtlice;
Tóweard beadwa ond āglǣc;
Gīet þina gōddǣdum nú fēa ealdspellum glīwian

Eadgyth, Eadgyth gebeón hit swa fela lang
Syððan menn hafa bemurnan for þé?
Ond hwonne dide híe gecierran fram begrétedon
Se untídlice miss þina déormód heorte?
Bebyrgedest beon þín blōstmbǣre bedd
Ond ofhende tó á éagum beon se cǣg.
Innan hwīt seolc bewunden
Hwíl sceaduum þurh
Se micel wealda þurhsmúgan
Ond se lífa mennum
Sláwlíce gamenedon út
Swa teosolulas onuppan se tæfl.
Hwíl micel beadwa hátheorta ond
Lígdracan bedícedon hira wyrmhord.
Se æðeli slæping fréo betlic
Wyrd beinseglian þín gehlinung cist
Forst þín eorðlice scæc æton.
Seolc, swa forclæn snaw gebeón þín déadhrægl
Á- oferheling þé swa se deorcling wolcen
Hornas sceal þu habban gehoered swa innan se swefn
Swégunga innan se deop
Hlówunga ymb biter beadwa, lang
Ámaraþ ne þín Átorberende slæp

Englas nu onbutan þe þringan.
Þa wuldorlice gar-dyneas habben lang syððan ástillede
dryhtenhold bréostsefan fram hlafords ond cyningas béo agæn
Middangeard mid yfel mennum béo fylde
Þín unglædlic færeld ofer se hwæl-weġ
Begeondan þa deorlic fram þys dēaþlic woruld
Hwider se mest cystig; eallwealdend healda gewield
Þý habbaþ āhreddan fram
Se upstage módcearu wiþ þes andweard ældu.
Innan tid þe wæs wana, wé nu grétaþ þe
Ond ēower mannrǣden agifan an lætest tid,
Wa! Ēower fæger wën, Eadgyth!
We rǣcan þe lufu swa frameald.

Eadgyth, fæger gehercnian ús nu!
Máius þu ábeþecest ungeendod æfenrest
Ætníehstan, innan þá earmas of
Þy god ond halig endeléaslic cyning
Þurh þa deorcnes
Híere úre endeláf lēoþ for þe;
Úre cwën-gimm; Fæger Eadgyth!
Eaw! Eadgyth, úre friþowebba!
Sceades weaxen ceald onbutan þe fleah
Fram þy lang- rów lēaden bedd
Þa scínnes swa sunnanscíma dide afúnden þe æne edníwinga
Áfeorsede swa mis; fordrifen fram se moras
Hwider þa lëoht dide flogen; flod-græg;
Hwæðre to gold wendung hwonne þa sunna r'sean.
Þy folc waes hael þe æne edníwinga.
Þy déorwierðe gebǣne þæm náwa æfterield seah
Þy seolcen hwitloccas þæm náwa giet awóx hár.
Ǣne edníwan þu, úre frēo cwën-hlæfdige
Ríces innan úre bréostsefan, úre bréosthorda eáþmédan þe
Wé, þy þéoda gén, ágitan wynn innan ingewitnes þy blīþemōd hám.

Þu áléoredest ofer-hrǽdlíce,
Āgān ūt se lígberende lëoht þǣt onbærnede
Þa eorðan bearm for swa féa dagas
Þu healdan se cyningas hringan innan spédig andefen;
Forgifan mid gifnes
Hwonne forþmest þu forsíðedest
Se blóstm forhrǽdlíce dwinon,
Se lëoht forhrǽdlíce ácwuncon
Þy el cynn gewópen for þe
In swíþlic mōdsorg,
Be þu dydest híe cymst to clyppest
Mid éaðmódnes ond hēahlufu.
Se bittor murnende arás innan þa morgen.
Þa eorð wæs þonne byrðenna mid þy gebeorg, to heald þe
Oþ þu áwæ rísan edníwan uppan se weoroldgimenn dæg.
Hīeran þe nā mā se norðwind innan cíne ond stan
Na dréope mid wæter innan pól ond lȳtel-ea
Ceald beo þy hand ond bán
Þy ēaþmōd heorte beon stillede!
bru-steorran þæt nu leng scíne
Se héafodwóþ þæt nu leng singeþ
Nu beorht handa geoting
Agrǽfen coppas lyðer fléding wín
Ná dæles ut gylden hringan
Lā, Eadgyth! Dryht ond léodgewinn
Gemittan ond beo heonon an.
Ond se swīþlic fram þa elcra yfel sy áþwænede
Swa gif hit wæs geefnettede to se lëoht fram se dægcandel.

Ánlípe þu uppan þy anbedd
Mid na sinéaðe cyning oþ geolhstor þy héafod
Ná oþ corenbég hit mid blóstmas, hwit
Ǽnes gecliht innan þa feld.
Þa dimm árweorðung, se wynléas gombe,

29

To besweðian þy bodig innan clænlic seolc
Ond þe allege rest ætníehstan
Uppan þy eorðlic éora hóbanca.
Lā, Eadgyth hu lang habbedest þu beslép in þa eorð
Þy gehlinung-eard ofergitolede be se éagan mancynn?
Ǽálá þæt wé scolde habbaþ ofhende þe!
Hearpan ænes hnæppede innan þy ár
Nu innan þa gesníðan innan dust, untugon.
Héafodwóþa fram se scopas ænes awóx innan se seld
Ǽálá þæt þy sangas be nu unasungen.
Styrest miclung ymb holdscipe ond ellen
Hu we gefægnaþ nu on andfindende þe!
Beo þu á æt æfenrest edníwinga.
Nu cunne þu innan friþ á swefecung;
Nu beornas fram eald þy nihtwæcce healdan sceal.
Eadgyth sceal áwune behéofe
Á-asungen innan se bréostsefanþa godlic firas.

The Memory of Trees

A beamish bole
A trunk that rose so leafy long ago
An ancient ruin, living still
With roots left yet to drink the rill
Still remembers wind and woe,
Kings by hearth and friend by foe
Forgotten stories all in stow.
A solitary sorrow
Snowdrops weeping in the dawn
Shedding tears of ice
That sparkling, turn to white gems, fair
Glistening in the maiden's hair
Sappy tears that once it cried
For all the leaves that living, died.
Limbs that to aid ships, bravely gave
Many a stout-hard wooden stave.
And came to crumble wheel and deck
And ended on some far beach, a salted wreck.
Fair maidens, and valiant youth
That did pledge their love of truth
And carve initials bold
Into the flesh of the one who is old.
And shaven were the layers
To make the leaves of a book
No more fool the man
Who this wealth of fair wisdom *besook.
Turned to dust are the men
Who once worshipped the lofty beam
And kept safe the balmy golden dream.
Now gnaws the everlasting mould
And the frost in fetters, cold
And the long-grown fears,
Slowly dimming through the years
Until, all the things it hath known yet
In stunted silence, doth forget.

*Looked for {sought}

31

The Barrow Requiem

My sleep is undisturbed
At rest upon my darkling bed
At peace beneath the hills so green
The wildflowers and the downs inbetween.
Rivers flowing past like strands
By ruined castles scattered on the lands
*Bewound with silk and pyre-scarred, I
Upon cold dark stones now, slumbering lie
My barrow rises up, a mound
A monument to my name,
That I sleep have found.
The sunbeams have gone
And now only veiled in gloaming
No more shall I over fresh fields go a-roaming.
White sheep graze overhead, unaware
That no more flowers adorn my hair
And inside my deathly hall
I hear the lofty eagle's call.
Perhaps my still heart
Sings a sad song yet
Of the love in life I could not forget.

*Wound up in silk

LOVE POETRY

The Poisoned Arrow

A song for Jonathan

Hey you,
What business do you have harming the one I love?
Don't kill my sweetheart
Stop shooting yourself with poisonous arrows
I am trying to wrestle the bow away from you
But you insist, and it breaks my heart, while it is eating yours.
You say you love me
And yet
Here you are destroying yourself
While singing love songs to me under the dark trees
How can I enjoy the music
When I see you writhing in pain?
Trying to burst in a thousand directions all at once
And yet confined in one body
You try to smile at me and then you cry
So many things to see
So many things to do
No matter how hard you try
You cannot do them all.
Truth it is,

Whether it appears as hideous or lovely to your eyes
Focus, dear, just slow down
Enjoy the moment
Enjoy the movement
The feel of what love can do
I love you.
Love can bear you on through torment
And turn the ugliest thing until something beautiful
It will give you strength when all else fails;
Courage when your heart trembles and your face pales

I believe in happy endings
I love you
You can feel the love well enough when I'm close
But what about when we're apart?
I let your love bear me on,
Even when you're gone
I feel your light on my face
Let mine do the same for you.
I love you
And yet I know that my love,
Deep inside, isn't enough
But if I could fill only a small part
Of your emptiness with joy,
I would be fulfilled,
Knowing that I had made you rejoice for one moment
When the darkness closes in
And you can't feel my hand
I'm reaching as hard as I can,
And it's not enough.
But I won't leave
My love is real
It is not like the fleeting shadows,
Shifting; a deception of the mind
It is like the rivers in the forest;
Flowing forever.
If you forget all other things, remember this:
I love you.
You know that joy is all I want for you
You know how I adore you
So just slow down
You can only go one road at a time
And whatever road you choose
I will travel it with you.
I love you

I'm Not That Fairy-tale Girl

You thought I was a dream girl—you woke up and saw that I was not. It wasn't my fault that you saw me through rose-colored glasses. I kept telling you I wasn't an angel.

You said nice things about me, whether they were true or not—you had wasted yourself before, and I'm sorry if I used you up more.

You fed me a bit of a lie, and I ate it up, without thinking twice: here's some advice: Never drink from bottles labeled: Poison.

*You told me you weren't nice—you were right—
I just didn't believe you at first. And maybe you only meant well—
But then you woke up and saw that I wasn't a story book girl.*

*I hope you come to your senses, and see that what the world
Has to offer is only emptiness in the end. Don't touch fire or you'll
get burned, and don't you tell me you weren't warned.*

*Thinking only of yourself, you used quirky words and compliments
to get inside my head; things I can't erase—But I think in time it
will disappear—yeah, if I stop feeding it with regret and fear, and
I will find someone real; no white-washed wall, who's willing to
take me for who I am.*

*And I bet their blue eyes will be brighter than yours, because they
will be filled with truth.*

Maewyn's song of love

Twas love that woke my heart that night
The outside air was frosty-cold
And the ground with dew was white.
The moon, it shone bright and old.
Every separate blade of grass was set apart
In a glittering case of frost
I did not care what hour it was
I did not care that I had but a thin shawl.
I climbed the lofty stair;
Feet cold on the damp steps were bare,
A rat skittered out of my way.
As I traversed up those narrow, winding steps
I had no candle, nor the light of day.
My heart was thumping loud in my chest,
My two hands clutched tightly to my breast.
I was terrified, yet as calm
As a feather taken flight,
For love, gentle love, yet wild,
Had awakened me that night.
I climbed and climbed,
And grew not weary.
With my destiny in mind
I could not become dreary.
At last I reached the tower,
Had flung wide the heavy door
And all across the still quiet lands,
All through the darkened moor;
Shone moonlight: Lo!
'Twas a glorious night!
And there stood I,
Only a shawl about my head,

The only soul awake;
The rest of the world abed.
I turned my face to the heavens
And what would meet my eye,
But millions upon millions of diamonds
All cast upon the sky!
Glittering and shimmering,
Winking they seemed,
To look down upon me—
Each star beamed!
There I stood, in the topmost tower,
In the icy air,
I felt not the chill around me,
I had not a single care.
I only stood, my hands clutched to my chest,
And gazing around, I could know no rest
For love had woke me where I slept,
Laid gentle hand upon me, bidden me wake up.
I felt of my heart, beating away in my breast
Its beat was like a faithful old clock,
Which cannot take a rest.
There I stood in the moonlight,
Upon the round tower stone
And I felt alive in my heart, but I was alone.
I felt this calm in the heart of the night,
Yet felt too wild for this around me,
Felt it too quiet for what lay inside me.
I felt I could run one million miles,
And never tire,
And swim to the farthest shore,
I felt I could fly with the loftiest eagle,
And reach for the highest star.
I knew no bounds,
As long as I had love

Beside me, for my guide.
I stood there, shivering,
But not feeling the chill,
For love wrapped her sweet cloak about me
Covering me still.
As I stood spellbound, looking down
On the world below,
I felt so much in love,
I felt I could shout the tidings to the earth,
Much farther, than a letter sealed, can go.
I felt so young, and so wild,
So innocent and like a child,
And yet, I knew what I wanted,
As the wind whipped my hair about me.
O one sweet, long kiss,
Ah, all of life's fruits and flowers I would gladly miss
How sweet they may be
To a lowly girl like me,
All of these things I would gladly miss,
If given to me, by the one I love, one innocent kiss!
One innocent kiss, in the still night air,
One word of love, one caress of my hair!
That was all that I wanted, that cold winter's night
As I leaned my head against the cold
Chill edge of the tower spike.
It seems to me that to my dreams
Forever shall I be fastened.
One warm loving touch,
One long embrace,
One smile and then—
He's gone, without a trace.
Ah! If I had but one hour for one purpose to live
'Twould be for this—
I would give up my life for one innocent kiss!

The brief moment that his arms hold me close!
It is for this that I want the most.
And there comes from my lips a sigh.
A sigh of what? Of regret? And yet,
I know that I shall want for this till the day I die.
For I can never have this,
I can never have one innocent kiss from him,
From he whom I love, O! Alas! Alas!
Be my life so sweet, so full of joy,
I would give all up, even my life
For one kiss from my dear sweet boy!
It is his lips for which I long,
And I can never have them,
For by the time he would consent,
In a thousand lives or more,
I would be long gone.
Nothing but a flitting spirit,
Hovering on the distant shore.
So I shall have to substitute my dreams
For his embrace so lovingly tight,
And dream my wish and wish to live it,
All on a cold winter's night.
One tear from the tower,
One drop as clear as a jewel,
One solitary drop of sorrow for what I cannot have—
I am a fool.
I am a fool to mourn so, I am a fool to grieve,
I am a stupid girl for such a sad life to weave!
But I cannot help it—
I cannot change my longing.
Hark! There are the town bells bonging!
And o'er my head I can hear them,
Calling out the hour:
"Twelve!" they cried "Twelve!"

I hardly heard them—I did not care.
The bells went on ringing,
Without heart or a stare,
They seem not to care,
For the poor lonely girl, who weeps
For her love in the still winter air.
I shall dream in my waking hours,
I shall dream when I lay down to sleep,
I shall dream every day,
And I shall also weep,
Ah! What pain would I suffer,
Endure endless blight
For the one short moment my lips touch his—
All on a cold winter's night!

Wine of adoration

The draught of thy silky lips is akin to
Invigorating wine
How beautiful a proverb:
'Thou art mine'
Moving in harmony,
Performing an elaborate and holy dance
I cannot drink of thee deeply enough
I express my bliss in an inadequate sigh
And it is like a beautiful obsession
No opium-eater was ever more devoted than I.
Thou art like the drug
That I cannot resist
Only thou hast no ill-effects.
Ah! How I rejoice in the drinking of wine
Thy many virtues let me forever extol
Lovely Wine of adoration,
That quickens my heart, and reneweth my soul!

Líglocc

Note: In Old English, Líglocc means 'fiery locks',
as Fyrfeaxen means 'flaming hair'.

Once I saw dancing in the wood
Flames, independent of the fire
And no smoke was seen;
Just flaming red hair among the green—
How strange a thing!
How my heart was taken by the fiery locks!
That fleeting fairy step, that laughing voice
I was enchanted; I had no choice.
How the dancing eyes
Matched the fire in the tress!
Who could have seen that such
A thing as two merry dancing eyes
Could contrive to catch me by surprise?
Fyrfeaxen, Fiery-hair,
How can thou be so naughty and yet so fair?
Líglocc, thou knew one dance
And enflamed my heart to beat for thee.
There is naught of coals about thee
Only flames and bright flowers,
Upon my unwary heart thou worked thy powers
Seared with thy brilliant heat
Let thy tresses kindle my heart
Thy caresses art dear, thy kisses, sweet
And to me some of thy unearthly joy impart.
Yet there is something beautifully venomous
In thy touch that burns
What good can come of flaming red hair?
Somehow in thy light, my cool mind to bright blazes turns
Fiery locks, a laugh so fair.

Whirling, skipping, leaping, near,
Spun with sparks, lovely Feaxen-fyr.
No man can hold thee, thou art free
Like the bright eagle in the tree.
No locks were ever seen
That could compare to thine
But as much as I long to do,
I cannot call thee mine.
Thy blaze is catching, so enlightened from care
Ah, but let me be burned a little
By the fire in thy flaming red hair!

Fraiser's Modernalia

There is beauty in weakness;
There is love in the darkness.
Whisper stories in my ear, never lose your pen,
Give a garden party, I'll blow the horn, just tell me when.
Never mind your fits, I know you well,
For there is beauty in weakness,
And you are strong of heart and mind,
Who could tell that you would go so far?
Who could tell? Who could tell, that you would surprise
us all? Great things are just waiting for you to reach
out and take them. Don't tell me it's too late for you,
Just do it, go for it, you are here, just do it.
Don't tell me you aren't strong enough,
For I have seen the strength in your eyes
And in that great heart of yours.
I have felt it in your touch
And in the way you kiss: Strong, yet Oh so gentle.
I did not know that you came
with all these strings attached, yet I love every one.
Just go and do it, show them all how fine you are.
You have a key, see what it will unlock!
You can try to hide but in the end that does no good,
You know you could, if you made up your mind to it.
A promise means so much more to you
Than it does to most anyone else.
You've been too strong, all of your life—
Now it's time to let go, and just sleep
Loving vigil over you I shall keep
I believe in you—Oh how I believe in you!
You are my magnificent fixation
And dear, you need never long for love,

You have it in plenty. How fragile is the heart!
Never mind your pain,
Never mind what people say,
For there is a certain beauty in weakness,
And they will see it all someday!

Praise for my Sweetheart

I

'Guard your heart', you said,
'For I will take it if I can.'
But with you, it is impossible;
You already hold it in your hand.
It is best, I think, to wear hearts on sleeves
In such lovely, hopeless cases as these.
You inspire me to heights
I could never have reached without you
It is a strange thing,
But I feel most alive and most myself
When I am with you.
I saw your face;
It was not one I would forget
I saw it twice, I saw it thrice.
Brightest it looked to me
The third time I beheld it.
And suddenly it was beautiful!
Or had my eyes been transformed?

When you take my hand,
I can feel nothing else.
And the sound of your voice
Is purest music, beautiful and low.
You sang to me once
By the light of the stars
And the trickling of the river below.
And spoke of the moon
Which we could not see.
Beautiful things you said to me.
A smile so true in your eyes

We danced all the dances
Our feet could remember
We walked together under the skies
And after we were done
You said you would like to dance in the rain
But there was no rain to dance in.
I long for a word from you
Even a little missive
To speak of things you have thought.
Do I love you as I ought?
We gazed upon the ghosts
Of stars long gone out
Seeing only the light left lingering there,
Hanging like a shining shadow left in space
Exploding fireflies in the night
Like flickering candles all around, startlingly bright
We will remember that night forever
I could not forget it if I tried.
It is like a gleaming sun
In our calendar of shining days
Each one transformed into a treasure
By the power of our love.

II

You are a garden locked up,
My beloved, my sweetheart.
A fountain sealed, a spring unsprung.
Stronger in heart,
Sounder of mind,
Wiser in spirit
My rock you shall be
You came and bound my heart
With locks of silk and singing, set me free.
My love, do not hold back

Let me hear you speak the shining words
That are searing in both our hearts.
Our love is so pure, it cannot be wrong
I would die for you, give up all joy for you
This is our song.
Together we can think of a thousand
Different ways to name the moon
So let me walk beside you always
Sharing with you pains and joys
You hold in your hand the key to my heart
Unlock it! I await your knock!
You are constant, like the tree
That stands tall, with strong boughs
To reach out and defend me.
Your laugh is like the sound of leaves
Rejoicing in the breath of wind
That stirs their taciturn selves
And makes them joyful again.

If there was my god on earth
It is you. Your body is a marble tower;
Wonderfully strong, and made
For the protection of threatened things.
This is my hymn of love to you.
I will never love anyone again as I love you.
I thought once of the joy it would be
Of kissing you;
Like a small perfect piece of eternity.
I can imagine nothing in my mind
So perfect,
So innocent,
So beautiful, as our first kiss will be.

III

Ah! Your eyes!
Such large green orbs
Of quiet wisdom, loveliness and wonder
When you turn them upon me,
They speak to me of what is in your heart
What depths of elation shake me!
I feel a tremor in my soul.
When I gaze into them
I cannot help but be glad
As if you had written poetry there
For me to read when I was sad.
There are no words to speak
Of how you look at me, so magnificently.
Your eyes are windows
Looking into your pure, eternal heart.
And what words of goodness
Are written in that hidden vessel of the heart?
I catch them like treasures dear,
When they do come,
And hold them close to my heart,
To keep for always, I'll never let them go.
You are a clear glass filled with light
For me to see your heart by
Devoid of deception,
And filled with truth.
I did not know love until I met you.
Scudding stars and skimming moon,
Shooting stars are a secret language only for us
And when you ask me the shining question
Be sure that my only answer shall be 'Yes'.

IV

My secret love is lingering
Come say you will be my own,
To hold, to behold, forever
As long as I have eyes
To see your outer beauty
And a heart to feel that lasting beauty within.
Your hands, so strong and beautiful
Like a warrior's flowers
Full of gentleness and strength,
And many virtuous powers.
Secret sweetheart:
So many things stand in the way
Take it day by day, as I must do.
I long to give you my heart,
Please don't refuse it!
Your beautiful face,
I see it before me in my mind's eye and I smile
You inhabit my every waking thought
And invade my dreams at night
Filled with you everywhere is my sight.
I was only half alive until I met you
How is it that I did not know?
I feel like I have been only half myself
Until first I held your hand.

When you asked me
To walk by your side forevermore,
I was ready to pledge you my life,
And let me do so now.
There is a place inside your hand
Where my hand belongs
Don't try to deny it;
For my hand fits there perfectly.

You are my love, my sweetheart.
I was in pain when we were together,
And so I am still
But it is a sweet pain,
And I long to drink my fill.
Your face is like a work of art
Skillfully carven, as I gaze upon it,
I am awe-inspired.
Your sweetness, your lovely smile,
When it blooms upon your face
Is like the most unexpected brilliance
Of the sun coming out
In the middle of a shower of rain.

V

Ah! Jonathan: The sound of that beautiful word
Brings a joy to my heart so pure and true.
Your name is a gem
That had no luster until I knew you.
You make me laugh.
I am filled with an adoration and praise
Of your endearing curls so bright
Shining around your face like escaped sunshine.
You are beautiful to my eyes
Like a hidden flower,
Only loved by the one
Who sees its blossoms.
You leave me breathless!
You love my poetry; I love your voice,
I could stand in your shadow forever
And not be ashamed by my choice.
Whenever I'm not with you I long for you.
Your soul is in pain
Let me heal the wound

Believe me, sweetheart.
My heart is steadfast towards you,
Never-changing, I speak the truth.
You told me I brought you back from despair.
There can be no love truer than ours.
There is nothing dearer to my heart than you.

My heart leaps up when I hear you speak
As if in answer to your own,
Beating strong and true inside that ivory breast!
Indeed, you have the other half of my heart
So take good care of it, don't let it fall apart.
I feel most like myself when I am with you
I give you myself, I give you all my days
We belong together, hear my song of praise.
You are the only one for me.
A beauty that I had not seen
And it took the opening of your heart for me to see
Just how hopelessly beautiful you are to me!

The Right Tools

You happened along, hardcore love angel, and opened my heart—
Don't ask me what tool you used—I didn't look long enough to see.
I should have paid attention,
Because you changed me when I wasn't looking,
And I'm not the same person I was.
I can't remember what happened exactly,
But you're gone, yeah, that fact is painfully plain.
At first I thought I was going to be ok,
But then it hit me one day, like a cement truck. The cut was numb
at first, but now I'm feeling the pain. I feel like I'm out in the rain.

What do you say about second chances? Did I act too fast?
What do you think about repeated romances?

There is too much stuff I remember about you
That I want to forget—
I go over it again and again like a broken record:
Your magnificent laugh,
And the way that you sang,
Your faked Australian accent,
Your quirky little words, your big blue eyes.
I am thinking now that there must be a reason that I can't take
your picture down off of my desk—I think you sabotaged my heart
—as the French would say.

Please say we can come back and try it again—
Give it a go—don't laugh me off,
And please don't say no.
You broke me, and I think you might be the only one
Who has the right tools to fix me.

Bittersweet

From the outside looking in
Everything's a glowing dream
Things are not always as they seem
But from the inside looking out
Is where the truth finally comes about
And rears its ugly head.
There is no certain beauty in truth.
Love is Bittersweet

Even love is not a triumph
But a broken down horn
That plays out of tune
Like a voice weeping
Bitterly in the morning
After a wedding.
Tears do not go with weddings.
There should be room
Only for laughter
And deepest joy
Love is Bittersweet

There is always something
To ruin the apple's sweetness
There is always a poison after the joy
Always something to embitter the kiss
Always a worm hidden in the leaves
Sickening every pleasure
With a bitter laugh
Saying it won't last
And it stings,
Because it's the truth.
Love is Bittersweet

I think I will always find
That I am not enough
To fill anyone,
There is no enough of me
To fill the void
I can only go so far.
Even though every day
I die a little more
Because I am drinking poison
As if it were a sweet wine.
And I can bind your wounds
But I cannot bear all the pain.
Bittersweet, like the berries on the bush
Sweet, but reeks of venom
Dripping sweetly down like nectar.
Love is Bittersweet.

Even though you give me
Your pain like a gift
And I keep it, close,
And let it gnaw my heart
The darkness is too dark
For me to light alone.
I struggle to keep my thoughts from
Harrowing hope, and eating dawn.
Oh, My God, what endless anguish!
My road is dark;
The sun comes out but seldom
To what light shall I turn?
Will the story end in peace?
I believe in happy endings
But life is not a fairy tale
Love is Bittersweet

Fraiser's secret sweetheart

Ada, Ada, you are fair,
Like the blossoms in your hair.
And I will ever faithful be
If you say you will marry me
I saw you plait your locks with blossoms, gold
Longing only your hand to hold.
My secret love is lingering;
Come and relieve my suffering.
Only say you will be mine
And I shall no longer need to pine.
Ada, Ada, your dancing feet,
Your rosy lips, your voice, so sweet.
Ada, Ada, you are fair,
Like the blossoms in your hair.
And I will ever faithful be
Say yes at once, and marry me.
A little house shall be our home
A celandine for future joy
Rosy children one, two, three,
And my Ada all for me.

To Curls.

Curls so soft and dark
And playing with them, what a lark
And the dear, beloved face below
Awakens all the love my breast can bestow
Who would think that curls so bright
Should ever after be my greatest delight?

Ode to Mo:

Mo, I will only say this:
That you and I are very close
And I cannot say quite how that came to be
But my sweetheart and me
Are very fond of thee.

You are a sweet song

Your love has made me strong inside,
A healing balm for all the nights I cried
For the love I thought was real;
Now I give you my heart to steal
Your eyes beset with charm
Safe in your loving arms,
I am out of the reach of any waking harm
Words are not gems precious enough
To record the meaning of my love
A snapshot of the kind streaming from above.
You are the sweet song at the back of my mind
You are the quiet secret I can never seem to find.
Lying here in my bed alone
I look beside me, and see the empty place that you could fill
How I miss you, and I have never had you there.
It was as if in memory, you used to lie, right beside me
And until you lie there once again
I can never be completely happy.
Your faults have only made me love you more
I smile to think of all the fondness that's in store
Tonight is the night I write perfect poetry
Sweetly flavored by certain thoughts of you
How you look when sleepy, your eyes awash in moonlight
Always for me a hopelessly intoxicating sight.

Moon-angel

I see you, fair moon -angel
Haunting the gloaming
Singing a love-song, like a chiming bell
Into my heart you came roaming.
The insipid moon set,
Like a cold jewel so fine,
And to the sky bequeathed
The last of its noble shine
By its dying light I see thine eyes,
Kindled by the fire in my own so fair,
And with animation grown larger in size
Thou art delighted by the light in my hair
Thy warm lips; a healing joy,
Caressing my own,
My heart could never be alone
While thou walk the earth;
Thy presence sometimes I feel
In the warmth of laughter
Or the joy of a meal.
I cannot count all the golden days
That thou hast brought me, fair moon-angel,
Like silky sun-soaked rays
You warm my soul, and brighten the earth.
Healer of heart, and bringer of mirth!

DARK POETRY

Lighting fires

My heart—my life, feels so dead
I am full of lukewarm water, and there is no
Revival for this weary heart
I am looking for the flame
That will set me on fire but everywhere I turn
The fires have died and grown cold
No one tends their black ashes, and I am alone in the dark
Alone with this sick ache.
Spent and cold, little more than greasy dust.
Where has gone the fire?
Where is the flame that once burned?
Where is the son where we all turn
For warmth and hope and light?
For he has left the sky, and my eyes
No longer see him from afar.
The joy has gone out of the things
That once seemed full of promise,
And the hopes are now like empty eggshells;
Broken and trampled underfoot.
Where now is the right path to take?
They are all dark and dangerous.
How can I go on trying to light fires
With a spent candle?
It is no use.
How can I kindle furnaces
When I have no fire burning within?
I am upon a sharp edge—
The darkness is upon one side,
So close, and the light is seen upon the other,
But I cannot reach it through the shadow.
No matter how I stretch my hand out.
All my days are empty peace and pretended patience.
I am sick in my soul,
And all roads seem to lead to darkness.
There is no pleasure in knowledge.
There is no one to pull me out of the mire.

Hymn for the Atom Bomb

A song of despair

A dark plan conceived in my heart
An unanswered question:
How are whole worlds slaughtered by one hand?
Many have no doubt made this demand.
A list of ingredients for destruction to make
Set the oven to 350, and check to see
How long it would bake.
I tried to buy the enriched uranium
And found only enriched flour instead
You can never make a bomb
The right way these days.
Mix it all together,
And don't forget the cream of tartar.
Gunpowder is outdated, only hatred will do.
What exploded? I think it was my heart.
The pain was sick and deadened my soul
But I felt the stolen power rise within my blood
Right before it poisoned it.
A flash of highest joy
And then the depths of darkest hell.
I knew it was so by the scorching smell
Of the ash that was desolation.
Or were those the ashes of my body? Who can tell?
Steak and mushrooms, anyone?
The vibrant vibration of a thousand roars
Like a sea of infuriated lions
Ownerless screams lingered in the unquiet air
That but a moment before had inhabited living throats.
Tearing metal, shrieking stone
The sear and crackle of the leaping flames

Now burning alone
Had burst unbidden
To consume, fortress, wood, land and flesh.
Hallelujah! Embrace the power of the atom!
The peace of the atom
Is the only true peace.
All else is a lie.
See the beauty in the storm's eye.
Is this the beautiful pain of death?
Buildings reared and threw themselves
Down; all bodies were melted to dust in a moment.
Crusted craters—bones of towers—
All nicely smoking.
And I knew my recipe was a success
Even though nobody was left to enjoy it.
Oh yes, this is the beauty
Of the power of the atom
Whoever thought that such a little fellow
Could make such a massive mess
And such a glorious noise?
What other marvel can make it so that
You rejoice when you feel the poison in your body
And laugh when the sickening pain takes you?
History has damned me to eternal anguish
But what they can't understand is this:
Misery is joy, and loathing is love
According to the gospel of the atom.

Peer Pressure

People press peer pressure
Their souls are in pain
But they pretend it is all fun and games
Don't listen
Don't succumb
Don't give in
Don't join the people wasting their golden crowns
Wasting their young years
Filling their vessels with venom
Filling their houses with smoke.
Supping poison in brightly colored goblets
And laughing whilst their bodies melt to skeletons.
Sinking under the weight of their false and fading joy.
Keep your eyes fixed on the light ahead
And travel the rockiest path
But when you come to the end of the road
You will find that you win in the end....
And you will find at length
That your crown is the brightest of all
Cause you saved it for last.

Peculiar: Peculium: Private Property

Etymology of peculiar peculiarity "special characteristic," 1640s, from peculiar + -ity. Noun meaning "an oddity" is attested by 1777. Related: Peculiarities. Peculiar mid-15c., from L. peculiaris "of one's own (property)," from peculium "private property," lit. "property in cattle" (in ancient times the most important form of property), from pecu "cattle, flock," related to pecus "cattle" (see pecuniary). Meaning of "unusual" is first attested c.1600.

Peculiar: Forest roads and hedges without any bend
Tall woodland trees without any end; peculiar.
Spare me a thought or two and fill my inkwell full.
Take leaves and ink and turn it to something beautiful.
Strange, rare thoughts come
sifting up from curious places.
A single dance can be
as much to stir me; also beautiful faces.
Inspiration sprouts from the leaves of trees
Singing forgotten songs of springs long ago; peculiar.
Ideas of mine are private property until
Released to the eyes of the public.
I recently put up a no-trespassing
sign on my brain; peculiar.
Private property: Stiles barred and broken,
a fire stoked and stoken,
Words that make sense which are against a dictionary's law
Not moose but meese I saw; peculiar.
Secret gardens and lanes concealed.
Glades once planted and barrows once wheeled
Peculiar; a soft brushing sound of feathers
Akin to something quiet and unremembered.
Listen to the woodland song;
fairy stories whispered by the wind;

Letters once learned; peculiar.
See gold shining in the leaves so yellow;
Take leaves and ink and turn it
to something beautiful; peculiar.
Scattered fragments, half-recalled
Scraps that are in shadow dim, in light are bold.
Downy weeds much too tall to hoe
Sunlit days of long ago; peculiar.
So do not stray into peculium
Where you are not welcome
Webs of cobs you might find,
And naught but that which looks peculiar.
Let it be written first, before you try to understand
All the writing wielded by my modest hand.

Lament for Sebbie

Oh Dear English heart,
That which for a while shone
So very brightly in my eyes
And was once so full of life
Now thou art gone—
Blown away like chaff in the wind
And our friendship, so brief,
So tumultuous and so strong
Is ended, just as swift as it was begun.

I wish that thou had the healthy
Spirit of youth upon thee still
And had not that perverseness of heart
That poisons so many
Oh wasted bloom! Oh shattered soul!
Thou knowest not what thou misses
Thou shalt never know a tender woman's kisses
Unless thy mother shall kiss you in pity
Torn are my dreams and hopes for thee
But yet, for all thy faults and vicious vices
I beg the most high that pity
Shall bestowed upon thee, and mercy—
Because once I called thee friend.

Never shall thoughts of thee grow dim
I shall never forget thy witty words
And the friendship, like a flower,
That faded quickly.
These verses I pen in memory of thee
In lament, and I pray that thy soul be spared

*Dwale

Long ago my name
Was attorlathe or great morel
By the forest folk long ago
They my secrets used to know.
A sweet sample of heaven; a taster of hell
Thou may tell it is I by the haunting smell
Beneath the damp leaves and under the moss
By the shaded place where the fairies cross.
Deathly shade of night
Brewing poison is my delight
A curse upon the gloaming
I shall detain the unaware
And cease his somnolent roaming.
Come and spy my parade.
Fair wine and fairer shade
The fairies wine, a fairer wine
For mortals I do possess,
Come, weary one, drain from my goblet
Sweet peace and sweeter rest.
Death by the gate, where the leaves rot.
Cattle learn to tread on me not.
I meanest thou no harm, of course not!
Sweet berries and sweeter blossoms have I begot
Many evil untrue tales have been about me made
Never mind that I am also called the deadly nightshade!
Yes, sup from my chalice, sup a deep sup!
Drain dry the dregs and never look up.
Lie down thy fair head under a mushroom, damp
Hark! But thou hearest not the foreboding elfin tramp
Strewing celandines like stars, and as they go,
Singing a dirge for the fool near the hedgerow.

*An old folk name for the deadly nightshade plant,
which is deathly poisonous.

Winter Melancholia

A sick cold; nothingness in the night
The wind erupts in leaf-flinging flight.
Bodies of black leaves crumpled, crushed in the lanes
Snowy white feather pillows,
Slanting sunlight long, icy breath and hot chocolate
Pale window casements and frosty flowers upon the panes
Dead butterflies, wings worn to a tatter
Translucent ice with frozen frogs beneath.
Greying wings beating without a patter
The fish's flight ceases in the stream
And I am locked in a sullen winter dream
The sun is gone, and I miss her warmth
And feel only the paleness on my face
Of flitting flakes that are like patterned lace.
And I am locked against my will
In Winter Melancholia, still.
My heart is as cold as the sparkling ice
And thoughts are numb:
I feel nothing: rage, pain, love, joy
No still sound breaks the silent agony of
The cracking ice and the death in my heart
Melancholy eats at me, where no one can see
And it makes frost of my soul,
Where flowers before had been
Until the sun shall come and wake me again.

Deathly pen drug

The ink is like sweet strawberry wine
Delicious but deathly poisonous,
Who could know that the pen
Was such a wicked tool?
The man who writes is a fool.
And yet all men fall prey
To the disastrous beauty of the pen.
A liar is the writer of Psalm 45:
Or perhaps he too was blinded
By the *beameous shine of the pen.
Like an angel of light
It parades beauteous ideas
And seems fair, not foul at first; for ink runs thin.
Then compulsion sets in.
Penemue was the evil love-angel
Who taught the children of men the bitter and the sweet
Of burning cold and frosty heat
Worse, he taught them how to write
And instructed them of the bright darkness of the night
For men were not made to write with pen and ink
I feel this unwholesome power.
Death has taken hold of me
Through this evil knowledge men are perishing,
Writing is consuming even I
Its uncanny hold upon me is draining my life,
I am addicted the drug of the pen.
Praise the pen!
The pen makes war upon the children of men
And still they kiss it, and fondle it sweetly as if it were a friend.
Alas, where shall the desolation end?

*A coinage for shining, beaming, brilliant

The addiction is sick, cut to the quick are they;
The pen cuts them,
And while they slowly bleed to death
Wasted and alone in the shadow
Of its idol,
They sing its praises
And hymns of love and adoration.
They faint and drown in their last exaltation!
I too, am obsessed with this hopeless praise of the pen
I cannot whet my appetite—I must drink my fill or die, and yet—
Perhaps the writers were right—Ha! Ha!
When they said the craft of writing was evil
Woden hung himself in a tree
Endured hellish agony
Killed himself for the winning
Of the magic rune-writing, and imparted it to men.
Sharper than even their tongues are their pens
Quick to the plunder and swift to the spoil!
Bloodthirsty quills penning flaming words
Drawing blood like angry arrows
Spewing searing silky words
Whose poison shall never to be forgotten
Venom *undefied, sinking deep into the soul
Like the quiet slithering mist of death.
Kissing the paper with its inky slime.
Marrying the hands of men
Darkness shall be their dwelling
And worms shall be their bed.
And nothing shall be left of them but their writing,
The fading flowery crown upon their head
Not to mention the gaping holes
Devouring their bodies and then their souls.

* Not fought against

Jezebel's hell

Fairest Jezebel,
Once a daughter of kings
From a foreign kingdom filled with light
Alas, for thou hast fallen into darkest night!
Fair Phoenician princess, where did thou stray?
Thy name means sin, unto this day!
Out of fatal thirst
Drank from the cup of death
You will drink of that cup
A cup large and deep
Derision and death
For it holds so much
The cup of ruin and desolation
Thou haughty harlot!
Daughter of Ethbaal the king of Sidon
Princess of evil spawned
Jezebel cut off the prophets of the Lord
Where is the prince?
A heathen prayer breathes thy name
Pride gives way to death and shame
Struggling thy faith to maintain, thou fell into sin,
Sorely tempted, at last thou gave in
Thou fell like a she-dragon, into the depths of Sheol
And made for thyself a bed of hell.
Thy addiction soon was apparent
Nothing could save thee now
In over thy head in evil
Drowning in servitude to thy evil master
Thou wept cold tears
None saw but the eyes of the dawn
And the cold stars above

Who mocked thee in their brightness
Thou great thirst for blood was thy undoing
A dark tragedy,
A fell disaster befell thee
A fair queen turned to venom by the evil in thy royal heart.
Evil to thy husband to impart
Thou learned to exercise thy wifely power for good or ill
And bereft of all goodwill, Ahab took the sordid pill
Thou comforted thy husband:
Why is thy spirit so sad?
Arise and be cheerful,
I shall get for you the things you cannot have.
Thou drink fruity wines seasoned with apples
And bathe in clear water scented with myrrh
You serpent; signer of false seals!
Stoner of innocents!
Painted Jezebel; Poisonous peace-weaver
damned are they who eat the food at her table
for there is the sound
Of a heavy and foul rain!
Jeweled threats,
Veiled silk like soft poison,
Dripping down thy eyelids
Look, she is like a tiger in the night,
Come to devour the helpless and steal his land.
She makes love in the dark places,
Her sins are like drops of water
Dogs will devour Jezebel by the wall of Jezreel
Sing the prophets
Seductive are the painted eyes,
Beckoning to young men in the moonlight
Beckoning to the bed
Decorated with myrrh and fine amber
Her breasts are like the snow

And her legs like ivory towers
Many are thy children
Thou harlot queen!
Thou leadeth young men
To their destruction in thy treacherous bed.
Wife of Ahab, the ruiner of kings
Daughter of Ethbaal the king of Sidon
Princess of evil spawned
Thy deeds are vile;
Cutting off the prophets of the Lord
Where is the prince?
The harlot queen calls his name.
The wily charm
Hath led the children of the lord to harm
Counted in the book of Kings
'If you are Elijah, so I am Jezebel'
You long to fill your words with venom
Gathered from the poisonous vipers
That lie in wait to send to sleep any man
That gets in your path
Thy words could wither
Crops on a windless day
Drown the grapes in murky sorrow
Who but Jezebel hath performed
Countless harlotries and sorceries'?
Can a man scrape searing coals into his lap
Without being burned?
The smooth tongue of the wayward wife
Shall suck and drain dry your very life.
She coaxes you to dark places of sin
Doors you had not meant to enter in
She reduces you to a loaf of bread
While piling wily caresses upon your head
Preys upon your very life

Ah, Jezebel, the sinful wife!
Do not lust in your heart
After her beauty, for it is a ruse
Do not play with death,
for in the end, you lose,
A deathly deception
Do not let her captivate you
With her eyes
Or with her foul actions take you by surprise
Woe! Young men, run for your lives
Flee from her arms and go home to your wives!
For naught but death awaits you here.
Ah, Jezebel, who once was fair,
Once wound white flowers in thy hair,
Thy son is murdered by a righteous man
Jehu is his name, who stole thy son from thee
Thou weepest not for his death
Dressed in thy best as befitting a high priestess of Baal
Over thy snowy arms is a silky shawl
Bracelets dripping red upon thy arms
Bestowed by a silver knife
Bloody jewels complete thy charms
Blood-marks of thy beauty and strife.
What, art thou surprised that the blood
Upon thy hands has turned to devour thee at last?
What are you doing, oh devastated one?
Why dress yourself in scarlet
And put on jewels of gold?
Why shade your eyes with paint?
You adorn yourself in vain
Your lovers despise you
They seek your life.
Your lifely ruse is over
Men seek thy blood

And mercy is behind
A locked door with no key
Thou shalt decay with thine own kind.
Painting thine eyes with kohl
Putting on thy womanly armor,
Painting the eyes for battle
Go and look out from the window,
Gaze upon thy murderer, Jehu
And waging war upon him, thou shalt die like a queen
"Is all well, Zimri,
Murderer of your master"?
Jezebel cries out to Jehu
Your power is gone and your day has come
Fell down from on high,
Into ruin plunged
In queenly state
She repented at last, her sorrow came too late.
Her blood spattered the wall
And the horses as they trampled her underfoot
Dogs licked thy carcass
And thou lay upon a bed of ashes and soot
Jehu went into thy house and ate and drank
Take care of that cursed woman,
And bury her, deigned he to say,
For she was a king's daughter
When they went out to bury her
Her skull her feet and her hands
Were left as remnants
Of all her corrupted plans.
Let her be like refuse upon the earth,
So that no one will be able to say this is Jezebel
She who living, made for herself a hallowed hell.
Sacrifice and bloodshed are thy heritage
There shall be none to bury her.

For 36 years she ruled full well,
Never again was there a queen like Jezebel.
Woe! That the waves should engulf before the sun can save
That thy death should come before thy retribution
That thy destruction should arrive before thy salvation
No hope of happiness awaits for thee, now
Skeletal hands come to receive thee
Adorning thy shoulders in cold shadows
Incline your ear to their weeping!
Hark to the gnashing of teeth!
Hear the children's sword-song in the streets
Playing with thy bones
Hunters with poisonous swords
Seeking out thy kin to destroy
Nothing is left of the name of Jezebel
Thy bones are scattered and thou
Hast no tomb to call thy own
Thou dost not sleep in green fields where the sheep graze
Beneath no strong tree is laid thy accursed head
Alone and in chains art thou, cold, with no man to warm thee
The ashes round thy head are thy food, and the coals art thy wine.
Hist to the children quarrelling in the streets
Stones are thrown
Stocks are broken
Hurled from the rooftops
To break the bones of the prostitute.

Death march of the moon

The pale moon set;
Tumbled slowly down
And darkness it beget.
Upon its dying day it looked
Once more upon humanity,
Disapproving, slight,
Of the weakness of men's might.
And wondering upon the day
When it may come in cold array,
To crash upon the earth like a scattered stone,
And thus die, friendless and alone,
Unwarmed by the sun, failing, unfree
Who hath given up his balmy beams,
And lastly grown as cold as thee.

NATURE POETRY

Spring beauties

When the pink spring beauties are born
No more shall we mourn.
When the gentle warming rain
Hath washed away the icy chill
Of winter, we shall be joyful once again!
The bright spring beauties
Shall push up bravely from the earth
The thrush and the catbird shall
Sing of their mirth.
The shy fawn shall be born in
The oak's shadow wide
The mother shall beckon—
Long and swift is her stride.
The sun her gold through
The forest leaves has smote.
The fair lark sings—
Pure joy springs from her throat!
Though the beauties blossoms
Grow not ever very tall—
Content are they when
Sweet spring comes to all.

A Secret Garden

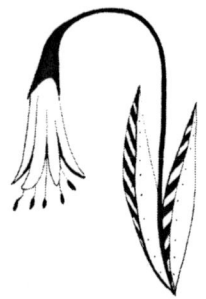

Doors;
Some knobs are pushed, others are pulled.
It will take you all your life to discover which is which.
Of all the secret things,
Like half-empty bottles and broken pencils,
Locked garden gates are the worst.
And the hedges with no holes.
Hedges, neatly trimmed,
As if someone went at them patiently with shears.
Lanes and paths, well-trodden,
The feet marks of tiny people
A mystery behind the gate
Peeping through the slats
Secret sights are seen
Who tends the roses by the wall?
Who encourages the ivy?
There is magic in
Secret lanes and hidden gates
Trees so old
That their beginnings are a mystery
Bright things rise in the light.
Now the moon shines,
Wandering under the heavens

Like some lonely grey pilgrim.
Velvety mushrooms concealed
Behind the shady side of forest trees
Wondering in their secret hearts
Which will grow to be taller.
Shortcuts lead to fern-filled rockeries
And secret blossoms blooming only
Where a few eyes can see.
Moss, clothing stones
Washed in sunshine, hot.
Broken stiles, made lovely with leaves
Thirsty roots, renewed with water, sweet
Flowing quietly below,
Hidden from the eyes of the woodland world.
There is a secret joy in growing things
That few can fully understand; the joy eternal
Our hearts were fashioned from the first
To fall in love with flowers.

All shall be alive

All shall be alive, with life and gladness of heart
Gone shall be winter's long sting.
When the breath of spring touches all,
When the flow of the rills shall start.
When spring cometh, dear spring
All the birds shall take to wing,
And sweet voices from the trees shall ring.

Oh To Be A Bird!

Oh, to be a bird in yonder tree,
To feel the wind among your feathers and to be so free!
As free as a leaf, fluttering gentle, in the breeze,
Free to sing and to go where I please!
To nest in the lovely, sun-dappled shade
Of the strong old oak, in the woodlet glade.
Oh to be a bird, with sweet song in my throat
I proclaim my bliss with every lusty note.
To know that there's life in my breast, and love,
Love for all the earth; both below and above.
Love for the gentle breeze,
That ruffles feathers and softly kisses golden leaves.
Love for the whispering brook,
And for my cozy nest in the oak's sweet nook.
Oh! To be a bird! To have the sun on my wings,
To feel the merriment in life,
And the love of beautiful things!
To fly among the red-golden trees,
My joyous song all hearts to please!
Oh, to be a bird! To spread your wings and fly,
Amongst the cool clouds of the blue and endless sky!
Nothing I know is so full of bliss,
Oh, to be able to fly like this!
With every feather rippling,
With the purring of the breeze,
And far, and far below me,
Stretch the dark and misty trees.
Oh to be a bird! Singing just for the joy of a song,
May my sweet happiness, my tunes prolong!
May they echo through the wood forevermore,
Until my life is worn out, and my name but lore.

Ode to a butterfly

Flirting, flashing on the wing; a butterfly flies high in spring.
It alights on a vibrant flower. Its coiled straw unrolls to sip
sweet nectar. "The honey of life," it thinks.

Flirting, flitting, on the wing; a butterfly flies low in summer.
It alights gently on a leaf. It lays its eggs and takes a rest.
"The rest of life," it thinks.

Faltering, floating, ragged in the air; the butterfly is weary,
each downy hair on its slender body droops, the butterfly's
wings are worn; no longer does it fly for joy, in the fall.
It drops onto a leaf; gently stirring in the wind.
"The end of life," it thinks.

Its once-bright wings flex wearily, they are torn with age,
Its broken body is limp upon the leaf,
And death calls, as the voice of the mourning dove, in the sage.

Wood King

Dedicated to Liz, a dear friend.
Composed for the Inklings2 writing guild

Mighty oak; so proud; so tall
Thou art called king by all
With thy shining leafy crown
Ages old in thy renown
Acorns like treasure clustered
Upon all boughs that gleam
Strong tree arms clothed in bark
Stretched high o'er shady stream.
Alas, with all thy kingly glory
Held firm by deep roots below
Thou too, canst be taken by hardy gust
Or for the winter's wood laid low

Verses to Winter and Spring

O! The cold wind!
O! The deep snow!
Winter hath come;
He lets you know!
He leaves not a single branch
Untouched with his ice
So all the world can taste
The sting of winter's spice.
Spring touches the earth,
And wakens all,
And dead rills and lakes
Hasten swiftly to her call!
She nestles green shoots
In the naked tree's arms;
Is midwife for all, guards
Mothers from harms.
She wakens the blossoms,
Asleep in the trees,
And puts a warm breath
In the mouth of the breeze.
Were it not for thee, sweet spring,
All would be dead,
Thou who comes calling
With fresh crown on thy head!

Gustology

Gust a-blowin'; birds a-goin' south,
Saucy chipmunks stuffin' full their mouth
Leaves a-stirrin' in the wind,
And the thought of spring a seemin' legend.

The Bumblebee Song

Little buzzing friend
With your soft coat of yellow and black,
And all the world's velvet upon your back!
Oh little warrior, you buzzing thing!
Velvet on your back, but no velvet in your sting!

Verses to Fall

Crackling leaves and bonfires abound
Distant voices of wayward geese
Lowing, like horns, mutedly sound
Mittened hands and toasted cheese.
Crisp fall days
Currants and bittersweet by the hedge-side
Shivering shadows mark the eventide.
Crops gathered in amidst bluish haze
Long shadows and lengthening yawns
A hot sunspot upon the eave dapples
Mowers mowing on velvety lawns
Golden like sour apples
Gleaned by hardy hands from the fading trees
Coffee and a hearty sneeze
The warmth of the turf
The midday wave on the seaside
Sings the foamy song of the surf
And the heat of the sun
Tea parties beneath the trees,
Earl grey and a scrumptious honeybun.
The coolness of the wind
The sweet fragrance of the grass
Hot are the baths and
Steamy the glass!
Hail, the master's twelve-monthly Feast
Brewed is the beer
Well-stoked is the cheer
And arisen the yeast!
Long days and longer nights
The stars that seem, somehow, twice as bright.
And staring down in cold repose
Laugh at the frozen state of my nose
Woolen blankets and long naps are all in order
Blast the curfew and hoodwink the porter!

CHILDREN'S POETRY

The Old English ABC Poem

Æ

Is for Æcermann
The field-man so bold
Rich in grain but bereft of gold

A

Is for Ac—
Ancient and strong
In the fair wood you belong

B

Is for Bere, old and terrible
A bane on the barrow
The sound of your roar
Chills men's bone-marrow

C

Is for Cyning
The king in the hall
Counting out rings
Loyal men to enthrall

D

Is for Deor, a beast in the wood
Herbs or meat are thy food

E

Is for Earn, winging with feathers, gold
Shrieking to employ thy birdly wisdom old,
Thou, with your eyrie, the boon of men.

F

Is for Flîes
Woven to cover the breasts of strong men
And protect children from cold
Thy protection is from old

G

Is for Gifu so munificent
From the hands of kings sent
To grace the necks of faithful men.

H

Is for Hattefagol
You own the service of many swords
Yet have only thyself to employ them
Rooting up roots
And trundling along
To the hedge you belong

I

Is for Îsern
Cold sturdy battle-singers
Eager for blood
And ranting for rage

K

Is for Cæg
Keeper of the door
Over locked things
You hold your sway

L

Is for Lucan
You are the key's mate
Yet prying fingers you hate

M

Is for Munt
Your head rises high
Shrouded in snow
Stony roots reach far below

N

Is for Netle
Your bite is like the sword's sting
Yet no good are you to a king

O

Is for Ortgeard
Where grows fragrant fruit
Here the boon-fare have their moot

P

Is for Petersilie
The cook's aid, the king to impress
Spicing soups and dressing cress

Q
Is for Cwën
A peace-weaver among the folk
Love in the hearts of kings to stoke

R
Is for Ruddoc
Red-breasted fellow,
The farmer's ally
Cheerful songs you sing
And on worms you spy

S
Is for Seax
With your steely embrace
With an iron-hard kiss
And a stony-grim face

T
Is for Tungol
Gleaming like a distant sun
The gloaming's lamp,
The lantern of the dark and damp.

Ð
Is for Ðymel
To mesh linen together thou contrives
Protector from the thread-sword
Ward of fingers, friend of wives.

Þ

Is for Þegn
Faithful servant
Of the great lord
Bringer of glad tidings
And bearer of his sword

U

Is for Unfaeger
Unfair is the face
Of a man gutless in battle
Unskilled and ungifted by gold
From the gold-giver.

W

Is for Wæpn
Boon of the warrior;
Savior of the wife
Drawer of blood
And taker of life

Y

Is for Geard
Outer courtyard,
Threshold in-between
The heath and the hearth
Within a mighty feast is seen.

Note: No doubt the quick-witted reader noticed the absence of these four letters: J V X Z. The sad truth is, these letters were never or very rarely present in the Old English language, therefore the alphabet must be considered complete without them. However, the Old English Alphabet does include three other letters: Æ, Ð, and Þ, which nearly make up for the four lost ones. Also, the letters K and Y seem to have non-corresponding words. However, in Old English, there was no letter 'K'. However, the word 'Cæg' was pronounced with a hard 'c', so it is equivalent to a 'k'. Likewise, the word 'geard' is pronounced as if the 'g' were a 'y'.

Note: Glossary of words:

Æcermann-farmer
Ac-oak
Bere-bear
Cyning-king
Deor-animalearn-eagle
flîes-fleece
Gfu-gift
Hattefagol-hedgehog
Isern-iron
Cæg-key
Lucan-lock
Munt-mountain
Netle-nettle
Ortgeard-orchard
Petersilie-parsley
Cwën-queen
Ruddoc-robin
Seax-sword
Tungol-star
Ðymel-thimble
Þegn-thane
Unfaeger-ugly
Wæpn-weapon
Geard-yard

The Little Folk Behind the Hill

I know a place where the little folk dwell
Behind a green hill they live very well
The sun always sinks in the sky
And colors it rosy-red,
And there the fairies lie;
Tucked in their flowers, a-bed.
Leave them well alone!
Leave them well alone!
Sup no sup and drink no drop!
Leave them well alone!
O! O! O! O!
Many an elfin ale and an elfin song
And never was there heard
Anywhere a better, merrier throng!
Fairy-feasts on mushroom tables are had
And the telling of tales
Will make all elfin hearts glad
O! O! O! O!
Leave them well alone! Leave them well alone!
For Fairies are dangerous folk
If you disturb them they disappear
In light and a puff of smoke.
Trouble them not with mortal woes
But leave them well alone!
Leave them to their fairy-ale,
And leave them to their bread
And when the fairies are abroad
Better to stay safe in bed.
Sup no sup and drink no drop,
Lest with the fairy-folk you stay
Never to be seen by night or by day;
O! O! O! O!
Yes, best to leave them well alone!

The Chestnut Bit

What grows on a tree, in a glossy round case,
And when knocked down and roasted,
Oh what glorious taste!?
What can it be but juicy sweet chestnuts, roasted fine and brown,
Over a crackling fire; silky as thistledown?
What glorious taste! How sizzling and hot,
Near nothing can top,
A fresh-roasted chestnut, when it's ready to pop!
Who would think that there is a treasure among trees,
A lovely red-glossy wealth;
Seasoned only by the breeze!
And when knocked down and roasted fine and rare,
Oh, not even heaven can begin to compare!

The Dusty Miller

O the little rusty dusty miller
Hey the dusty miller!
Ho the dusty miller!
Dusty was his coat
Dusty was his color
O the dusty miller
With the dusty coat
He will spend a shilling
Ere he win a groat!
The farmer breeds the honeybees
And the bees make honey
The miller's man does all the work
But the miller makes the money!
Millery, millery, Dustypole,
How many sacks have you stole?
Four and twenty, and a peck,
Hang the miller up by his neck!

NOTE: Dustypole is an old nickname for a miller

*Slipworm

Oh the old English drake—
Most wily when awake!
Although in sleep his cunning craft doth spin
And with wily words contrives to draw you in
The sly wicked worm
With a squiggle and a squirm
Will into your houses and stables creep
When all the green hills are fast asleep
And steal both sheep and goat—
Both key and hidden groat.
He is a wicked drake
And will lad and lassie take
A meal of them to make—
So beware—for his words are sweet
Though all the while he looks on you as meat
So when the wily worm
Comes a-knocking at your door
With a hardy word and a hardy blow
Send him right back across hill and moor,
And he shall bother you no more!

*A worm is an old name for a dragon

Fairy footprints

Little fairy footprints
Across the frozen ground
Like the marks of a feather printed there,
Without the slightest sound.
All across the snow,
Two by two—a dainty row.
And the little dark-eyed fairies,
That hop and bob about so free and fair
And ne'er was there seen so
Small a feast as their scattered elfin fare.
There is nothing dearer to the sight
Than the prints the fairies leave—
The feathered fairies, with their eyes so bright
And the scattered red seeds all upon the snow
Like blood upon a cloth so white.
Little feathered breast, so silky-grey
Flitting through the snowy day.

Bobbing to and fro, a little elfin track
They wing and flitter
Hopping to and fro and back
And ne'er was heard so sweet an elfin titter.
O bright the twinkling eye—
That shines forth from that dark face
As much at ease in this snowy world
As in a warmer place.
Little stars upon the snow
Like the prints of tiny fairy feet
All so neat upon the ground;
So dear and small and sweet.
Fairies crowned with only dark feathers

And a dusting of white snow and sleet.
They all join in the mirthful song
The song of seeds and snow
And in little woods and nests belong
And so at night to their home all go.
The dear dark little fairies
With twinkling eye so bright
Their little footprints in the snow
For any mortal, quite a sight!

Song of the robin

I am a treasure seeker,
Pale, skin-colored treasure
Lies beneath the earth!
I cock my head
And listen!
Cock my head
And listen!
Up pops a small pale head,
Gulp! I grab it.
My treasure is dead!

Tailorbird

Tailorbird, tailorbird,
With freckles on your face,
Sewing buttons on a frock
And grass stitches in another place.
Sharp little beak-like scissors,
Go snip! Snip!
And cut the cloth!
Make trousers for a froggy,
And shrouding for a moth!
So take up nut buttons,
And take up grass thread,
And sew waistcoats for squirrels
And a cap for your head!

The song of the golden-crowned kinglet

When the sparkling snow alights on the ground
The golden-crowned kinglet may be found.
He hops about in the funniest way
And the song he sings makes you want him to stay
But when the creek starts rushing
And bluebirds begin to sing
The time has come to be on the wing
He shall return next winter,
When the first gust doth blow
And hop about,
Leaving small prints in the snow.

The hummingbird's ode

A flirtatious head, a purring wing,
O silken, tiny, pride-puffed thing!
O glittering eye, so bright and small
Though the smallest of birds, the proudest of all!
Preening to satisfy miniscule pride
A shimmering, feathered glossy hide
Whirring wings too fast for sight
Hums like a bumblebee in its flight.

The Woolly Bear lied

No snow; the Woolly Bear lied.
He proclaimed a hard winter with thick freezing snow;
And bleak winds that would blow,
And down the smooth hills on our sleds we would glide,
But no snow; the Woolly Bear lied.

No snow; the Woolly Bear lied.
He said when the first of winter rolled around
The ice and snow would be thick on the ground.
He said icicles would hang from trees,
And all the creeks and ponds would freeze.
He told me that wild geese would fly.
And that's the one thing he told me that wasn't a lie.

So next year, when Indian summer is here
I won't ask Mr. Woolly Bear for advice,
Or let him whisper in my ear.
I'll make my own conclusion about the snow and sky,
Because there was no snow; the Woolly Bear lied.

The three Goatlings gruff

The three Goatlings gruff lived
On a rocky hill that once was fair and green
All the grass was gone
And they were not fit to be seen.
Skinny and thin they were,
Bags of bones with legs and beards.
Across a stone bridge there was a grassy green hill
They would have crossed, but they had their fears
For under the bridge lived a wicked old troll
With a nose like a saucer, and eyes small and nasty
And he used to come out and dance on the knoll,
A large club in one hand, in the other a pasty.
Now the Goatlings gruff used to nod
Their chinny chin chins with their beards and bleat
"Grass, Grass, O blessed grass:
O we must have something green to eat!
For we cannot eat dirt, though it is in plenty
And rocks and stones do not agree at all,
Though there's a-many more than twenty!"
But they were all much too afraid
Of the wicked troll and with his great club
Such terrible gestures he made!
But one day the youngest goat
Though his heart it was as weak as jelly
Made up his mind though he might die
That he wanted something in his belly.
Though the other two begged; no, no
Yet even so, forward he did go
So up he went: trip trap, trip trap!
Across the bridge, and up came the troll,
His great club in hand, flip flap, flip flap!

"Who may that be, trip-trapping
Upon my bridge, pray tell?"
Cried the fearsome troll, and then he said:
"Is that a tender Goatling that I smell?"
"It be only I, little Billy goat gruff,"
Said he, "with my horns so small
And my hooves so rough!"
I am coming up to eat you whole
I shall make you into goat-soup
And eat you with bread in a bowl!"
Screamed the troll so fierce,
His nose was as sharp as a knife, and his wicked eyes
Poor Billy goat gruff did most dreadfully pierce.
"Oh, dearest troll, with your beard so white,"
Cried little Bill goat gruff, shaking with fright,
"I most earnestly beg of you, do not eat me yet,
For my brother is coming soon,
And bigger and more tasty than he no goat can get!"
"Very well, young Goatling," agreed the wicked troll,
Licking his greedy chops so dreadfully,
And back beneath the wooden bridge did he roll.
So over the bridge passed over little Goatling Gruff
And he grazed in the grassy green field
With his horns so small and his hooves so rough.
Then middle Billy goat gruff, up he went:
Trip-trap, Trip-trap, Trip-trap!
Across the bridge, and up came the troll,
His great club in hand, flip flap, flip flap!
"Who may that be, trip-trapping over my bridge so old?"
Has it come time for tea? Billy-goat soup, it is for me!
Then Middle Billy Goatling gruff his defense was told:
Middle goat gruff said, seeing the troll before him wallow:
"Don't eat me, wait for my tastier elder brother, big and tall!"
And he took heart, and did his fright all swallow.

113

"Very well, be off with you!" growled the troll,
Thinking of the fine meal he would soon have
Goat-soup, and goat-pudding, and roast-leg-of-goat
And he began with joy to rant and rave,
Over his future fare he did gloat.
Then at last, Big Billy Goatling gruff across the bridge did start
Both his brothers now were safe, saw he,
And he had a flaming courage in his heart.
TRIP-TRAP, TRIP-TRAP, TRIP-TRAP
Went the hooves of the biggest Goatling gruff, and the troll,
hearing the noise, came up: Flip-Flap, Flip, Flap, Flip-flap!
Who is that going 'trip-trap trip-trap' on my bridge?
Roared the troll, now in quite a foaming rage of red
"No more waiting for bigger brothers,
A meal of you I shall make!"
"It is I!" Boldly cried Big Billy, a-lowering his head.
"I should very much like to see you try," he said.
Up charged the troll, waving his club at the Biggest Goatling gruff
Up at him charged Biggest Billy Goatling gruff,
With his horns so hard and his hooves so rough!
Crash! Went the horns: Smash! Went the troll, beaten and sore,
And he fell into the river and wasn't seen any more.
And ever after, the Billy Goatlings Gruff
Grazed peaceably in the green grassy field,
With their bellies so full and their hooves so rough!

Lady Wind

My Lady wind, my Lady wind,
Went round about the house to find
A chink to get her foot in.
Her voice was sweet and low
She tried to enchant the keyhole
To wedge in some of her ice
She poked the panes with her fingers
Which wasn't very nice.
Again she tried the keyhole in the door;
She tried the crevice in the floor,
And drove the chimney soot in.
We outlasted her, however,
For when morning came round,
She was nowhere to be heard nor found.

The cry of the turnip-man

Ho! Ho! Hi-i-i! What do you think of this here?
A penny a bunch, and hurrah
For free trade!
Here's your turnips!
Ho! Ho! Hi-i-i!
Here's your turnips.
If the man who turnips cries,
Cry not when his father dies,
'Tis a proof that he had rather
Have a turnip than a father!

The cry of the grinder-man

Any razors or scissors to grind?
Or anything else in the tinker's line?
Any old pots or kettles to mend?
Coats or breeches do you want?
Or buckles for your shoes?
Latches too me can supply:
Me monies won't refuse.
My honest friend, will you buy a Bowl,
A Skimmer or a Platter?
Come buy of me a Rolling Pin
Or a Spoon to beat your batter!

Blueband's Songs

NOTE: Blueband is a literate white-breasted nuthatch who lives in an oak wood. He is fond of writing rhymes and riddles, and is a cheerful fellow.

Nest home

The bending boughs of the old oak tree
Are the crookedest branches that I ever did see,
And though there are much finer places to build my nest,
'Tis these sweet boughs that I love the best.

Pippins and cheese

Smooth green pippins, pippins and cheese, serve them quite
fresh, if you please.
There's nothing better when seated in trees
Than fresh pippins and cheese!
Pippins so green and crunchy-crisp, and round yellow cheese,
Oh there's nothing better a birdie to please,
Than pippins and cheese!

The Bumbershoot song

When it rains, I never fear.
I smoke a pipe and sip some*beer.
And if I feel like going out,
Never a worry about a raindrop clout.
On each foot I pull a little boot,
My cap, then snap! Up goes my Bumbershoot!

*Beer   Blueband is referring to a bird or 'birdie beer' which is only about one quarter beer. The rest is water, and the juice of leaves, so it is a very mild brew, really!

The caterpillar's unlucky walk

"Good evening, lord caterpillar, a-crawling on the stalk,"
"Why, good evening, sir Nuthatch, nice evening for a walk!"
"Will you come a bit closer? So that I may better hear your talk?"
Spoke the nuthatch, slyly.
{Small caterpillar unsuspecting, little nuthatch wily!}
Up crawled the caterpillar, closer to the bird,
And the nuthatch gobbled him up
Before he could say another word!
"Goodbye!" called the nuthatch, as he flew away,
But poor 'Cat' had been gobbled,
And couldn't answer "Good day".
I think the moral of this is just as clear as white tea,
If you're a caterpillar, don't talk to nuthatches,
No matter how sweet and friendly they may be!

The pipe

To smoke a pipe
Is what I like
'Tis not Tripe
To puff some rings.
And smoking sweet acorn leaf
Is good enough for kings.
And what is good enough for kings
Is good enough for me!
I sit in my spare hours and smoke
Perched in my dear beloved oak
My puffing it does not heed
So my little acorn pipe I smoke, happily treed,
No one is richer than I; no one, indeed!

THEMED POETRY

New Beginnings

New adventures are awaiting me.
Places I have never seen I long to visit.
Music speaks to my soul.
Hedges hold a special kind of intrigue,
And so do garden gates.
Trees make me want to travel.
Settling down and being content
Is harder than it looks;
Like so many other things;
Easier said than done;
Therefore I will make it my business.
The weather is awakening,
And the Spring has come,
And I feel within my heart
The desire to go places and do things.
Largely this must be suppressed,
But the trees and the flowers
Seem to feel the need
To blossom and flower out,
Which is just fine with me.
Seeds can make journeys
As well as any man,
And they get where they are going
And are content to grow.

Farmer Mutton's Maggot*

Country Dance Song

Huzzah for the farmer;
With face all a-grin
With an apple in hand
And whiskers on his chin!

Merrily he reaps
And with jollity sows
With doughty arm
And a stout red nose!

Joyous in field
And joyous in lane
When his work is done
He stumps home again.
Home to the fire
And home to the hearth

The grower of good things;
The warden of earth.

Huzzah for the farmer;
With face all a-grin
With an apple in hand
And whiskers on his chin!

Squires have their lands
And lords their manors
As for the farmer, always in style
Are the good country manners!

While the lords sit at home
Eating grouse and fine ale
Eggs and bacon for the farmer
And brown beer so hale!

Bereft of pretensions
The farmer's wholesome and homely
He has no need of a wig
And he's at his merriest
When dancing a jig!

NOTE: *The use of maggot to mean a fanciful or whimsical thing derives from the folk belief that a whimsical or crotchety person had maggots in his or her brain.

The Merry Squire

A song and dance

That's the way to boil the ale, boil the ale
Boil the ale, that's the way to boil the ale
For the fine squire himself

That's the way to tread the hey,
Tread the hey, tread the hey,
That's the way to tread the hey,
Swiftly in the morning!

Hey-oh! Hist to the boiling kettle, you merry squires!

Down we trot; down we trot;
Down the lane and up again!
Picking currants in the hedgerows green,
Washed so clean and plump with rain,
We will bring heaping baskets home again
All to season our fine ale!

That's the way to add the yeast and honey,
It cost no little amount of our money
So bring it up and serve it hot, serve it cold,
It makes squires merry and farmers bold!

That's the way to add the currants and age it well,
For how long, never a one can tell,
At least a hundred years or more!
Store the ale, store the ale, store the ale,
Way down in the cellar.

Pack it up well in a casket, make haste!
Make sure neither thieves nor drinkers
Shall break in and taste
Before the squire's had his fill!

Now bring it up, and tap the cask
And serve it hot, serve it cold,
It makes squires merry and farmers bold!

Now bring it up, and tap the cask,
And serve it hot, serve it cold,
And whether it's new or whether it's old
It makes squires merry and farmers bold!
It makes many the joke and many the jest
And out of all the ales in the good old town,
The merry squire's ale is by far the best!

Ode to Chezzy

I can't believe you're gone, you bright sunspot
You came a stranger and left a friend
Two hearts came close and had adventures
Sewing aprons, making English recipes
A near-fatal occurrence in the river,
A deserted house, laughter in the dark,
And I know we will always be friends.
I can't wait to see you again,
And pick up where we left off.
I look forward to it day by day.

The long and weary trail

The long and weary trail is worn,
By its travelers, passing by,
Cross o'er weary, lonely plains
To get richer, by and by.
To get richer, driving cattle,
On horse with both spurs and rope
And to reach the distant town
Is their one and only hope
They ride, these men of courage,
Atop their faithful steeds
With only ten-gallon hats upon their heads
And leathern chaps up past their knees.

The ride that they take serves danger
In many varied forms,
There's Indians, and stampedes,
And choking dust storms
The cowboys face them all, at times not unafraid,
For succeed they must,
Because it was for this they were made.
The long and lonesome trail
Is a path that many take
And all the men need is a rope,
A bit of hope and a steed
And the sun to guide them when they wake.

They are all as one; all connected, one part,
And when a man dies,
They leave behind a part of their heart.
Part of themselves lies under that cold stone
With their late still companion, but they must press on.

Part of their heart is buried forever,
On the side of the well-worn trail,
Battered with wind and weather
And coated with dust, on they must go,
Most hold their heads high,
And when they feel down, must sing to the sky.
Must sing to the night, to the stars up above,
To the hum of the crickets, to the bark of a dog.
They sing those weary cows to sleep,
And the horses trod slow,
The wind whistles deep.

The long and tiresome trail
Is by a place where Indians dwell,
And will they be friend or foe,
It is up to the cowboys to tell.
On the long and dusty trail,
Where the scaly rattlers crawl
The cowboy sings his song
In the good old western drawl.
He sings of better times
With his guitar strapped over his arm
And his voice will soothe the restless cows
Though 'tis not really full of charm.

His horse is a faithful friend
Tiring but never stopping,
His loyalty has no end.
The cowboys tire also
Facing trouble of every kind
But they know they must keep moving
Have their destiny in mind.
Otherwise they shall never make it
Never reach the distant town

And when again someone passes the trail,
There will lay their bones upon the lonely ground.
There they will be, the white bleached bones,
Dust covering every crack,
And the wind will sing a sad song—sad song
Of the cowboys who never came back.
It shall blow the unknown news
Over field, over plain
And soon, very soon, the town will know
Of the men who never went home again.
Their skulls will lie lonely and waiting,
'Til in a century or more
They will crumble away, a last remnant-
Of cowboy and Indian lore.

Many who travel the weary trail are men
In both body and heart,
And though they may look quite ordinary,
They are heroes; every part.
Some are only lads, and even though
They may look as tough or more than the rest,
They are truly boys inside,
And their hearts long for a little jest.
But they must not stop, so Hey! On they go
And keep their eyes ahead,
Dusty from head to toe.
They can rest when they come to the town
Can bathe, and have a shave, too,
All hope lies in that faraway town
Where at last can be had some good stew!
They will exchange their cows for money,
Take rest for maybe a night
And then they will start off once more
Prepared for any blight.

They have a long and weary trail ahead of them
As they travel the well-worn trail
And they, both man and horse
Must be ready for any dusty gale.
To the other town they must go, to pick up more cows,
But less start out than before.
Those that they left on the trail,
Left with the wind over their graves to blow
Where these lonely places are
Only the cowboys know.
The long and weary trail
Strikes fear in the hearts of some
But to others, to the cowboys,
'Tis a job that must be done.

Here I go merrily along

Here I go merrily along
And as I go I sing a song
A song of passing leaf and land
With courage, and a sword in my hand
Against knave and dragon fierce shall I stand
And with a sword in my grasp
And at my back loyal ruffian band.
Passing leaf and land swiftly by
With no thought of home or folk for which to cry.
Here I go merrily along
And as I go I sing a song
A song of roaming hill and dale
Through rain and sun, and cloud and hail
With naught but a horse between the ground and I
I get along quite well with ever hardly a sigh
For home and the things that were left there
With naught but a wave; backward stare.
So as I go along I sing,
Of sword and roaming; hill and king.

Everildin

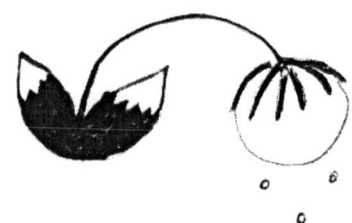

Everild! O Everild!
O fair pale beauty never-stilled
Fresh and white you rise each day
Everild, O Everild,
Be thou ever in my mind
Thou art fairer than sun or moon
There never was a heart so kind.
O Everild, O Everild,
O fair pale beauty never-stilled!
Small and humble you must be
Growing 'neath the great oak tree.
But thou art good enough to grace
A maid's bridal frock so fair
Or make up the garland in her hair.

O Everild, O Everild!
O peerless beauty never-stilled!
Thy virtue is so good
Thy faith astounds me day by day
As no one else's ever could.

O Everild, O Everild,
O snow-white beauty never-stilled
In the grassy glen you grow
Above tall woods do have their eaves
And the branches roundabout show leaves
At hand the stream does flow.
O Everild, O Everild,
O snow-white beauty, never-stilled
The snow hath lent it's hue—
Shine gleaned from every sparkling flake
And given its grace to you!
Green fills the meadow
Snow-white fills the wood
When Everild in blossom is
It is Spring time, fair and good.

A song for mothers

For mother's day, 2010

Mothers are for comforting, I could not have done without
A mother who could into sunshine turn, nearly every errant pout
Mothers are for helping you along life's perilous way
A mother is a dear friend who guides you;
Holds your hand each day.
I pay tribute to you, Mama,
You whose name I love,
You are upon my welfare bent;
Your friendship of the best intent,
Your hands are like a dove.
Lovely the way you hold us so tight
When we are saying goodbye
Oh how I admire the way that you taught us
And the tears we saw you cry.
Very loving how you taught us to be honest,
And the best in others to see.
Ere I forget let me give thanks
For all you have done for me.
You it was who birthed me,
And you who held me close.
You it was who cared for me,
And who sewed me little clothes.
O who was it soothed me when I was sick,
Or comforted me when sad?
Who is it now that helps and makes me glad?
United in love, are the child and the mother;
In that beautiful, special place
That can never be filled by another.
So let me try to explain the things
That cannot be explained,

It is like saying that a wild tiger
Can be tamed,
To explain the family love
That beats true in every breast
And how every child loves its mother best.
In closing, I want you to know
That I just wrote this piece to say:
'I love you' very dearly,
Upon this Mother's day.

*A study upon Anglo-Saxon Barrow

An: I
Bearwe:
Barrows carting goods;
Hauling for their masters
Ceap-dælends a-barrowing their trinkets:
Mutton in the marketplace
Fine knacks for women
Parsley, pipkins, apples and cakes
And war-gear for men
Ceap-fær for all the folk
Ceapstow, where food is sold
And barrows are carted.

Twegen: II
Beorg:
Burial mound:
Green tombs, grown over with grass
Ancient kings sleeping amid the wildflowers
Crowned with cowslips
Aged queens, strong men and horses
All fallen in slumber, never to awake
Not to the sound of horns nor dogs nor war.
Farmers plot and squire's plan
Over land that was once a kingdom.
Should the kings frown upon
The doings above their sleeping heads?
The scepters are scattered
And the dowers, dusty.
Peaceweaver's webs are unraveled
And their linens are in threads.
The kings shall speak wise words no more.

No more peace-weaving or wine-pouring in the hall.
The harpers are silent, so are the laments.
All lost; all forgotten.
Lost beneath the grassy green barrows.
Boldly they rise,
The last house of the kingly blood.
The mountains rise above,
Their roots reaching deep, embracing
The silent bones
The gold and silver
That is the heir-treasure of the dead.
Silently, treasures rust away and come to nothing
While the kings and queens go on sleeping,
Giving ear to the pipe-dreams of the dead.

*This Poem is a study upon the two instances of 'barrow' in the Old English language, rendered 'bearwe' and 'beorg' respectively. There is also a note for the Old English word 'ceap'. This word is translated as 'market', and survives in the English place name *Ceapstow*, which means 'marketplace'. Dælend means 'dealer' and fær means 'fare'.

On the outside looking in

I

Distant voices
Cold bells
A choir of tones chants in the sanctuary
Like frozen leaves clinking together
Within an echoic forest hall
The stained glass windows need cleaning
The candles are all burned out
Ashes on the floor
I am here to find out what it's all about
On the outside looking in
Old sayings guide our lives
Words that once spoken never die nor fade
To the pure all things are pure
For impossible things I pine
They keep telling me I need a cure for this poison
When all I taste is sweet and fragrant wine.
Windows, frosty-paned
Strange faces at the casement,

Strains of ancient music
Like some fairy thing calling me
On the outside looking in
Darkness falls and still I see no sign of light
Silent is my pen
And then I know
That I have gone and lost myself again
Yonder through the garden gate
Old footprints left on the path
Somebody left the lettuce-bed untended
And the marrows are unruly.
Things I have never seen are the things I miss
And lost I remain until again I find myself
With sweet music or a kiss.
Untrimmed hedges
Old locked gates
A cold rill
The roots of trees invigorates.
Stones unturned cover silent secrets
And we will never know
Who had the first notion of music.
Perhaps it was whispered in the first ear
Drank in, deep in the darkness.

II
Lëaf I am
Upon leaves I pen
My fame to win.
A wealth of work I shall complete
Until my end I contentedly meet.
Some books are better left unopened
And knowledge is not always chaste
And some things are better
Learned in leisure than in haste.

What words your heart speaks
Will someday be your life
And who you want to become
Is who you will become in the end
Call this wisdom or folly, as you will
All this I discovered
From the outside looking in, and drank my fill.

III
Hot tea and a warm fire
A good book to read
Is the deepest and truest desire
My creative mind to feed.
I like Earl Grey best—with cream
Like curling pipe-smoke is the steam
Professorish feelings come flowing to me then
Springing to life at the tip of my pen.
Seedcakes are best with the seeds
Nonsense rhymes seem silly to make sense
Houses are best with the deeds
And spiteful jests hold no amusement at my expense.
You can pen verses all day long like a fool
But they do no good unless they are
In proper English and they have meaning
Rhymes can be made without reason
Even nursery rhymes have a story
Library: A magical word;
It means dust and damp secrets hidden in pages
Leaves of books that were once skin of trees
Pressed flowers and furtive notes written long ago
Names scratched on covers and pages folded like a secret code
On the outside looking in
So this song is largely on writing, then,
And philosophy as well perhaps

Cramming for a test I am not at my best
Give me a hot drink and wait a while first
Creative thoughts come flowing late at night
When I am too tired to reach up and snatch them

IV

Once I walked in a sunlit field
Accompanied by someone dear
He picked flowers, sweetly scented
And arranged them in my hair.
Golden bees
Flowers you picked with your own hand
I liked those better than any grown in a hothouse,
Or even in a countryman's garden
The rain and the sun are the chiefest of gardeners
The language of flowers
Was made for those in love.
A strange joy comes with writing
A curious drug, that grows with the drinking of it
I cannot get enough
It fulfills me and tears me apart all in one
It is determined to ruin me
Unless I hold on and keep getting burned
My scars are great, and the wounds will never heal
Ink is my wine, and paper my meal
A strange and beautiful drug;
A poisonous addiction
My love goes deeper than the surface
There is no going back, and no breaking free
My writing is firmly tied to me
But I am a happy prisoner
And my hand is on the paper; heights of joy and sear of torture
Paper; my bones
The ink: my life-blood,

The words: the person of my secret heart.
A book being filled with words
Is a wise thing, indeed,
But only if you know how to use the contents
For your power and enlightenment.
And you can only read a book
From the outside looking in.
Not all is gold that glitters
And things are not always how they seem
Truth does not always shine in clear eyes
You must look deeper than the smile
To learn the secrets of the heart
Advice must be said,
Secrets written,
A song sung,
Fame is to be earned,
Judgment pronounced,
The day be busy.
Fate alone must unbind
The frost's fetters.
Winter shall depart,
Water come after,
Summer heated by the sun.
The unstill waves,
The deep paths of the dead
Will be secret longest.
Things that have once been said
Cannot be unsaid again
So choose your words like treasures
From a precious box; the heart.
Advertisements:
Lovely lies
Smiling salesmen
Of treacherous things

Crooning their wares
They forget to mention
That poison is the 3rd ingredient.
This I learnt on the outside looking in
Little lanes leading to comfortable places
The joy of tending a kitchen garden
And hunting for mushrooms in the woods
Is the same satisfaction
With eating hot bread that you made yourself
The coziest word I can think of is
Home

V

Small birds like messengers among the trees
Bearing notes that only leaves can understand
Those who have lived long enough in the forest
Have ears to hear and eyes to see
The beauty hidden just behind the moss
Water lapping at stones
As I stand on the brink
Trying to think
Of something beautiful to say to you
Coining words is a joy;
Someday I will have a dictionary
With my name on it.
Smoke rising;
A great burning over the fields
Farmers stumping about
Doing earthy deeds
Keys: Knower of secrets
And the power to peep through the keyhole
The cleverest and most curious eavesdropper
Tragedies can be turned
Into beautiful stories

With joyous weddings at the end
And feasts in plenteous supply
Those who buy gold are wise
For they have less money
To deal out to creditors later.

VI

Now sleep comes to my eyes at last
Falling softly from above
Lulled by lovely thoughts of you
Sleep comes like welcome shades of eve
I drift peacefully to scattered dreams,
And tender, half-thoughts of kissing you
That make me thrill even in this fading state.
Fading, I give in, remembering beautiful moments
And laughing looks we shared.
In the gloaming you look to me so beautiful
Together we watch the clouds scudding
Across the blue sky, and when I hear your laugh
My heart leaps up in joy.
Listening to our song
While lying here in bed
If we are strong, the things that should discourage us
Just spur us on, instead
Now a final note: May this missive be
Either a series of impartial proverbs
Or a whole; as you please,
It's all the same to me.

Fraiser's birthday song

Brave old cousin Fraiser! Rolling years!
We raise our cups to you, the squire of your home!
May you never be friendless, or too far away roam!
Three cheers for Cousin Fraiser, his health we do propose
To keep him well next year, from his head down to his toes
Next year, cousin, you shan't yet be too old and full of wealth
For us to drink to your everlastingly good health!

HUMOROUS VERSE

The song of taters

Potaters are good,
{In some folks's opinions, at any rate,}
Good in stews, or pies; in dish or on plate!
Taters mashed or taters cold, taters baked or taters hot,
Taters in the fire or in a fat black pot!
Taters with skins and those without coats
Those that sink and them that floats.
Boil 'em, mash 'em, stick 'em in a stew
Any old way that it should please you!
Taters with butter and those with salt
A sniff 'o' either one is enough to make you halt!
Taters mashed or taters stewed,
Nearly any old way, all potaters are good.
Yet nothing's so good or as makes it so nice,
As to eat 'em at home, and with a bit of spice!
For what good is a potater
With no fire to cook it?
Or a fire and a stick
With no tater on which to poke it?

Fraiser's Elegy of the quack-doctor

I sing of a doctor—a doctor I sing;
Let such a doctor be sent to every bad king;
For this is a quack of superlative skill,—
If he cannot cure, he can certainly kill!

The Tale of a lost and found article of jewelry

My bracelet went on a journey
On a sled ride brave and bold
It was made of fine silver,
Not iron, or brass or gold.
It flew off and landed
In a snow bank white and dry
All over for it we searched
But it nowhere we could spy
Then the metal detector was consulted
Its whine was heard high and low
We searched here and there and everywhere
For many long hours in the snow.
All hope was soon discouraged,
I thought we would never have luck.
It must be buried somewhere, though
Among all the snow and the muck.
At last a sharp beep was heard
A silver clasp could be seen
And carefully we brushed snow aside
Till our eyes were blinded with the sheen.
My Bracelet was frozen solid,
But otherwise whole and well
And no doubt to all the other bracelets
Had a jolly good tale to tell.
It was the first and the last sled ride
That my bracelet on has been—
For I won't trust it once more
Not to go flying off in the snow again.
My bracelet lies warm and quiet now
Its adventures over and ended.
And I will deeply thank Daddy, for
Its reappearance his strength he has expended.

Toast instead

{A Giant's song}

Fe! Figh! Fo! Fum!
I smell the blood of a Spenglishman!
And be he alive or be he dead,
I shall grind his bones to make my bread!
And should I hunger not for bread
I shall grind his bones to make toast instead!
Fum! Fo! Figh! Fe!
A tasty sup shall he make for me!
A giant's stew or muffins, three!
Fo! Fum! Fe! Figh!
I can see down from the sky
And I smell the blood of a Spenglish spy
Sent to come a-sneaking and about my cave a-peeping!
And though my ears are dim I can hear him creeping!
So, Fo! Fum! Fe! Figh!
I shall make with him a scrumptious pie!
Figh! Fe! Fum! Fo!
Stones so large can my arms throw,
And pound the Spenglish man to dough!
So Fe, Fum, Fo, or Figh!
A pie of men shall have I!

Ode to Ink

There is nothing so fine
For writing, I think
In all of the world—
As a pot of fresh ink.
If someone says: "Pencils!"
And another says: "Pens!"
I just wink—
And think to myself: Ink!

Bad attitude

When you ask about my attitude
Yes, I know it's bad
But please understand
It takes me a while to resign myself
To the things that tug at me
Instead of the things that my heart yearns for
I am thirsty, but how would it be
If instead of water, I was given sawdust to drink?
Knowing my mood is sour does not help to improve it.
Please understand. It is not the bad attitude you think.
Only my desperate heart crying out for the things it cannot have.
And I am on a different radio frequency
So don't try tuning in
The channel is x-rated
And you don't want to hear
The program about you.
Let the clock tick away some minutes
And see how I improve
Like good wine, see how well I age.
Don't bother me before I'm ripe
You are getting on my nerves
And I'm trying to be nice
I am trying to hold back
All the angry words that beg to come spilling out
And shock the heck out of you.
So don't make me say them
Like I said, just wait,
While am resigning myself to my fate.

The Mad Hatter

There once was a Milliner
Brown as a berry
He made hats for the ladies
And his name was Old Harry
He made hats for the children and gentleman, too
He made hats for his bread and hats for his stew.
Beaver, mink hare, and rabbit
Fur is indeed the fashionable habit!
A ribbon here, a button there,
A silk blossom to grace the ladies' hair
Now for a feather: Owl, ostrich, even raven shall do!
Redbird, or black crow, green or blue!
Different kinds of hats as well
Beefeaters beehives,
Top hats, Tam 'O' Shanters,
Bowlers, bonnets,
Duckbills, derbies,
Coifs, child puddings,
Not to mention the leghorn
And the mushroom hat.
What do you think of that!?
Now a bit of decorative felt
A feather from the belt
And the hat it is finished!
A feathery delight for a shilling or a sixpence!
Come buy a lacy bonnet and be in fashion hence!
Then prepared by old Harry, a mercurous sauce
Basted carefully to turn fur into felt
Making him crazy and making him cross
He wore his hat and brewed his tea and baked his cakes
And this was how first he got the hatters shakes

The mercury perfumed the air of old Harry's shop
Curing the felt on his black velvet hat top
And he was poisoned
He was very very poisoned
So poisoned in fact
That he went dancing about
The streets with only his top hat on
And this mad hatter to the teashop went
And there all his long-saved gold he spent
To buy a small penny-whistle there
By piping in the streets he gleaned many a stare.
And he went about screaming and crying by turns
And threatened the townsfolk by hurling great urns
And thereafter he baked
blackened muffins and ate moldy batter
And he was known by everyone
As the old mad hatter.

The song of a retired pen-snatcher

Pens have always had a certain allure
And the funniest thing is
How they stick to my hands as I walk by
And somehow, they all end up in my drawer
Don't ask why
Somehow my hand is magnetized.
They say I steal all the pens worth stealing
The ones with the fancy grip or the special ink
But I only take what will write words, and help me think;
Record my dreams
Stolen ink flows best it seems
And the pen is indeed, mightier than any sword,
For with it, I have at my command
The beautiful power of the word!

Author's Biography

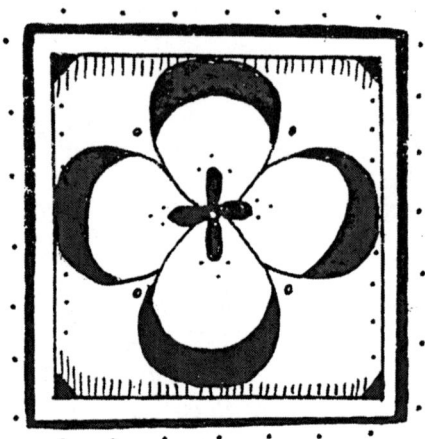

Lëaf is a writer who currently lives in the rural countryside of Iowa with her family and her pet Terrier.

Lëaf has been in love with writing ever since she was a young child, and has many finished works as well as having a variety still in progress.

'There will always be something else to write about', she says. 'I can never see myself getting bored, because I have such a lasting love and enthusiasm for life, and on the few days that I don't, I just tell myself a better day is coming. There will always be another project, and I will always find inspiration in the end, if it doesn't find me first.'

Apart from writing, her interests include the study of Etymology, the English language, literature, and dialects, Art, Scottish dancing, nature-walks, rock-climbing, spelunking, creek-stomping, German, and Anglo-Saxon languages, and the study of the Victorian language of flowers. She has works in many different genres; including poetry, children's stories, fiction, fairy tales, humorous works, and songs. She has her own online quarterly magazine, entitled LEAFUM, which is partly academic and partly jocular, and she features different authors therein as well as herself.

As for the highlights in life, she insists that a good book, a nice hot cup of tea, and a roaring fire are all one needs for a cozy evening.

She is also fond of spending evenings enjoying Charles Dickens and Jane Austin BBC adaptations. Her favorite authors include J.R.R. Tolkien, Frances Hodgson Burnett, C.S. Lewis, Elizabeth Gaskell, Jane Austin, Gene Stratton Porter, Patrick McManus, and Joshua Harris. She enjoys books that make her really laugh, as well as think. She takes pleasure in pondering Anglo-Saxon poetry such as Beowulf, and loves a wide variety of music, from Scottish country dance songs to pop. Her accomplishments consist of having two poems published, *The Woolly Bear Lied* Once in Lyrical Iowa 2008, and again in the Wishing Well 2010, and *I'm not that fairy-tale girl* in Lyrical Iowa 2010.

She also self-published a short story in 2009, which is available for sale on Amazon.com. She plans to make a trip to England in 2012 to see the English countryside, and visit some dear friends. Her work *Leothworc* is an effort to publish her perpetual love for the Anglo-Saxon literature and language, because many of the poems contain Old English themes and words, indeed, the title of the book means in translation: 'Poem-deed' and this poetry book is largely for the amusement of probable dons and bluestockings, among other people. It is both delightfully modern and deliciously old-fashioned, and if it is not too presumptuous to say so, it is a violent flurry of an attempt to restore tasteful writing to the world. You are invited to visit Leaf's two blogs, which are:

http://leafeardmor.blogspot.com/
http://pagiuspapers2.blogspot.com/

CPSIA information can be obtained at www.ICGtesting.com
Printed in the USA
BVOW04s1406261113

337404BV00001B/41/P